OVER THE HILL AND ROUND THE BEND

MY ADVENTURES ON A BIKE IN WALES

RICHARD GUISE

summersdale

OVER THE HILL AND ROUND THE BEND
Copyright © Richard Guise 2009

Summersdale Publishers Ltd
46 West Street
Chichester
West Sussex
PO19 1RP
UK

www.summersdale.com

Printed and bound in Great Britain

ISBN: 978-1-84024-743-5

Substantial discounts on bulk quantities of Summersdale books are available to corporations, professional associations and other organisations. For details telephone Summersdale Publishers on (+44-1243-771107), fax (+44-1243-786300) or email (nicky@summersdale.com).

OVER THE HILL
AND ROUND THE BEND

MISADVENTURES ON A BIKE IN WALES

*To my mother Nancy Quiningborough (1916–62),
who first took me to Wales*

Acknowledgements

Thanks to Jane Browning, Wynn Davies, James Faulkner, Roger Fox, Glyn and Alwena Williams and the Meteorological Office. Special thanks to Lucy York and Sarah Herman of Summersdale for keeping me on the straight and narrow and to Julie Challans for following me round the bend.

In January 2008, the University of Wales Press published *The Welsh Academy Encyclopaedia of Wales*. Within a month, my own copy formed a heavy and already well-thumbed presence on the desk. Much of the information in this book comes from that source and I gratefully acknowledge it. Wherever I refer simply to 'the *Encyclopaedia*', this is the book I mean. I don't know about its sales, but the *Encyclopaedia of Wales* is without doubt the best-*smelling* book I've owned.

Contents

Author's Note

Place Names
This book is written in English and therefore uses the English names or spellings of Welsh place names (where there is one), as used by the Ordnance Survey. For example, 'Hay-on-Wye' rather than Y Gelli Gandryll and 'River Dovey' rather than Afon Dyfi, but 'Caernarfon', as the former English 'Carnarvon' is no longer used. Any inconsistencies, for example in the hyphenation of place names, follow those used by the OS at the time of the ride.

Personal Names and Hotel Names
To save their blushes and my skin, some of the personal names used in this book are not their real ones. With one obvious exception, any names mentioned for accommodation and eateries, however, are the real ones.

The Four Compass-point Extremities of Wales

The four compass-point extremities of Wales, accessible without the use of a boat, are:

NORTH: near Llanlleiana Head, Anglesey
SOUTH: Rhoose Point, Vale of Glamorgan
EAST: near Biblins Bridge, Monmouthshire
WEST: Pen Dal-aderyn, Pembrokeshire

The east point is accessible by bicycle. The others are accessible only on foot.

Route Around Wales

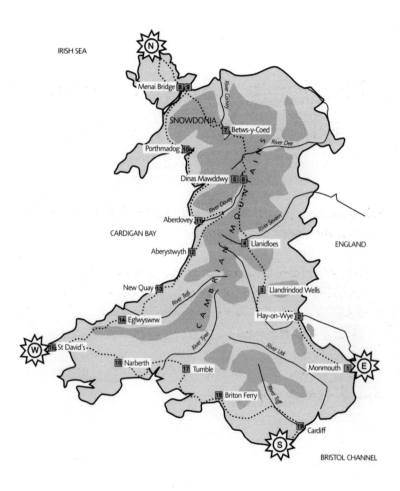

IRISH SEA

Menai Bridge 8 9

River Conwy

SNOWDONIA

7 Betws-y-Coed

River Dee

Porthmadog 10

Dinas Mawddwy 5 6

River Dovey

Aberdovey 11

River Severn

CARDIGAN BAY

4 Llanidloes

ENGLAND

Aberystwyth 12

CAMBRIAN MOUNTAINS

New Quay 13

River Teifi

3 Llandrindod Wells

14 Eglwyswrw

Hay-on-Wye 2

St David's 15

River Tywi

Narberth 16

17 Tumble

River Usk

Monmouth 1

18 Briton Ferry

River Taff

19 Cardiff

BRISTOL CHANNEL

Day 1

Keeping it Simple: East Point to Monmouth

Most cross it by car. Some by bus or train. Nineteenth-century linguist and walker George Borrow stepped down from his train to cross it on foot. I was about to cross it by bicycle.

For much of its length, the route of the English/Welsh border defies logic. Here in Monmouthshire it obediently follows the River Monnow en route to its confluence with the Wye until suddenly losing concentration, heading east, hitting the Wye at the wrong point, panicking, turning upstream instead of down, realising its mistake and then petulantly ploughing south again to disappear into the woods.

It was at this point of petulance on the left bank of the River Wye that I rested Tetley, my two-wheeled steed, against a newly erected signpost before crossing into Wales. On the riverbank a solitary robin danced among the bare branches, while the grey water below rearranged itself into a steady flow after its bristling encounter with the shallows upstream. The bank itself showed signs of recent winter floods – dark-brown mud deposits, dirty, straggled weeds, once-white plastic bags – while up beyond the path, early daffodils made hesitant yellow splashes amongst the dark greens of the wooded hillside. Above it all a bird of prey carved lazy patterns against the steel-grey sky.

Apart from the track, the bike and me, the signpost represented the only obvious intrusion by mankind. It said 'Symonds Yat 1½ miles' (behind me) and 'Monmouth 4 miles' (ahead). Nothing to indicate the border and nothing to reveal that this lonely spot is the easternmost point of Wales. Since I'd just spent half a day getting here, I found this a little strange and immediately wondered if the nation's other three extremities would likewise go unremarked.

Cycling to the four corners – the east-, north-, west- and southernmost spots – of Wales was my aim, and, if this anonymous start was anything to go by, perhaps I was the first to attempt it. At that moment I felt obliged to remind myself why. Pulling a Marmite sandwich out of the big, blue bike bag, I sat with my back against the spokes and peered along the invisible border.

Although some nights I've fallen asleep wishing I were Welsh, I wake up every morning to find that, inexplicably, I'm still English. Or, as the Welsh would call me, a *Saeson* – a Saxon. I tend to think of it as a strange land: tantalisingly familiar but inescapably strange. And yet is it that strange in reality? I can't count the number of times I've visited the country, stayed there – hell, I even lived there for three years – but maybe I'm out of date. Maybe twenty-first-century Wales has given up the struggle and, like so many other places, finally been swallowed up by the globalism of the times.

To find out if it really is such a strange land, I felt that I couldn't just retrace the traditional east–west forays so typical of the English. Nor should I simply follow the Welsh coastline, fabulous though it is: with its tourists, holiday homes and caravan sites, it can't be typical – and anyway, such a tour has been done before. I'd always felt that the real Wales was lying there waiting to be discovered, just off the main road, behind the tea rooms, down the track, up over the hill. And that another version of it lay somewhere in the urban and industrial fingers of the south. What I needed was a route that gave me a glimpse of all these faces of Wales: a customised Cambrian cocktail. It was with this in mind that I'd laid a map of the principality across the kitchen table and, with the help of my best high-tech gadgets – a wooden ruler, some string and four jam jars – identified the four extremities at the four compass points and connected them in a way that I hoped would take me on a satisfyingly serendipitous tour.

I'd take them in an anti-clockwise route, heading from here across country to the northernmost point at the tip of Anglesey; from there mostly along the beautiful coast of Cardigan Bay to Wales's westernmost point, which I'd assessed to be not quite St David's Head; and finally across the industrial heartland of the principality to Rhoose Point in the far south. It looked like nearly 600 miles, which, at my stately pace, meant around three weeks – surely enough to see if my view of Wales as a 'strange land' was still valid... if it ever was.

Having thus reminded myself of the answer to the 'Why am I doing this?' question, I saddled up, pointed myself at Anglesey and crunched across the border. Two days later I was to wonder if I'd phrased the question correctly.

The trail I was following was upgraded in 2007 and now forms the Peregrine Path, a route for walkers and cyclists along this stretch of the beautiful Wye Valley. It follows the trackbed of the old Ross and Monmouth Railway, opened in 1873, swallowed up by the Great Western and eventually closed in 1959 – even before the Beeching Axe could fall on it. Cycleways along disused railways always rate among my favourites – not just because of historical connections but due to the fact that cyclists of a certain age share with railway locomotives a significant preference: we don't care much for gradients.

The first feature on my ride was as sudden as it was unexpected: a heftily engineered pedestrian river crossing. Biblins Bridge is a narrow suspension bridge, fixed firmly to the banks by sturdy cables that easily coped with the weight of the three people walking carefully across it towards me. They'd clearly read the notice that warned 'running, bouncing and swaying could damage the bridge'; the bridge user too, I would guess. It led, they told me, to Biblins Holiday Camp, hidden in the trees on the Herefordshire bank.

A little further on, beyond a ruined cottage abandoned so long ago that the forest had almost swallowed it up, the river gorge opened out into a wide expanse of meadows, with sheep munching away in the foreground and, in the background, the A40 dual carriageway roaring the once-peaceful scene into immediate submission. From magic to tragic in fifty metres.

My map revealed that, just before the national boundary leapt out of the river and into the hills beyond the far bank, it made a tentative landing to capture a small white cottage for the Welsh, while leaving the grander house behind for the English. This seemed a suitably oddball introduction to Monmouthshire, historically an oddball county in itself.

Like that of any nation, the history of Wales can at first seem rather confusing and, to help me – while not, I hope, hindering you – here is a brazenly brief overview. (Historians, look away now.)

An Absurdly Simple History of Wales
(all dates approximate)

Phase 1: 250,000 BC to 600 BC. Someone lives here, but we're not sure who.
Phase 2: 600 BC onwards. Celts arrive from Central Europe, bringing their gods, druids and language. They never really leave.

Phase 3: 55 BC to AD 410. Romans come, see... and sort of conquer. Well, VII out of X for effort anyway.

Phase 4: 410 to 1066. Small, squabbling kingdoms. Award for Best Attempt at Unity goes to Gruffudd ap Llywelyn: whole country, six years. Runner up: Rhodri Mawr (Big Rod): most of the country, seven years – including defeat of Viking invaders.

Phase 5: 1066 to 1400s. English Normans try what they're best at: suppression. First attempt: virtually autonomous Marcher lordships in south and east, to keep unruly Welsh at bay in north and west. This shrunken Wales conquered from Gwynedd by Llywelyn ap Gruffudd (not to be confused with Gruffudd ap Llywelyn). Second attempt: Edward I of England eventually declares war on Wales, creating the western counties and going castle-mad. Meanwhile, in the non-violent world, Welsh literature flourishes.

Phase 6: 1400s. Owain Glyndŵr's rebellion against the English, including a temporary Welsh parliament. Military defeat.

Phase 7: 1500s. Political union with England. Eastern counties created.

Phase 8: 1800s. English go all romantic about Wales, while Welsh go all literary again – when they're not down new mines or in new factories.

Phase 9: 1900s. Industry declines while nationalist culture rises. Westminster governments fiddle with the counties. Welsh ask for their own assembly and get it.

Phase 10: 2000 to the present day. Welsh go back and ask for some powers for the assembly too. Welsh celebrity glut.

I intended to use this framework to help me keep a cool historical head while cycling through the Welsh landscape. Its first test would be to unravel the reason why some used to think that Monmouthshire was neither England nor Wales. It turns out to be simple… simple arithmetic, that is.

Wales's absorption into English control was a two-stage affair (Phases 5 and 7 above): eight counties in the thirteenth century and then five more in the sixteenth. Monmouthshire was one of the five counties created by Henry VIII from the problematic Marcher lordships, i.e. those along the border with England.

$$8 + 5 = 13$$

Thirteen was a tricky number for legal purposes, since English Common Law was to be administered by four 'circuits' that would each consist of three counties – no more, no less. (No, I don't know why either.)

$$4 \times 3 = 12$$

The odd one out was to be Monmouthshire. So, although it was politically and ecclesiastically part of Wales, legally it came under the jurisdiction of Westminster… and later, Oxford. This led to a tendency in some contexts to refer to 'Wales and Monmouthshire' as though they were somehow separate, which they weren't. The myth that they were, however, was exploited by some English newcomers to the county in the nineteenth century, when a slight detachment from 'Wales proper' was thought to enhance one's social status. A bit like living not in Brighton but in 'Hove, actually'.

In the 1974 rationalisation, Monmouthshire became Gwent, the name of an ancient Welsh kingdom in Phase 4. Since the 1996 *ir*rationalisation, Gwent has been split up into several authorities and the one of these that includes both my start point and the town of Monmouth is called… Monmouthshire.

My historical head was still cool.

Having passed the railway's old Hadnock Halt, the Peregrine Path wandered between a few industrial units before suddenly throwing me onto a busy bridge across the Wye and straight into Monmouth, a very small, old county town but, as we'll see later, by no means the smallest in Wales. Monmouth sits on a narrow peninsula between two rivers, but while the Wye dominates its eastern aspect, the town is named after the smaller Monnow which meanders in from the west. Monnow is an anglicisation of Mynwy, swift water; the town's Welsh name being Trefynwy, Mynwy-town. (Spelling of place names in this book follows those used by the Ordnance Survey, unless other information prompts a different spelling.)

As I pushed Tetley into the narrow streets, the modern noise of the A40 receded, to be replaced by the timeless noise of children bursting out of school. Two muddy, orange-jerseyed rugby players clattered along Glendower

Street and through a red front door; a spindly, blue-topped girl asked, 'Can we go round to Fiona's, mummy?' through the window of a badly parked Range Rover; a Welsh boy with a pink Mohican shared a lewd joke with his black-blazered mate; while an old man in cap and tweeds bent low to squint at the inscription beneath an ancient Indian Bean tree. Welcome to Wales.

I checked into my hotel on Agincourt Square, stored the bike, washed off the little dust that a four-mile spin had accumulated and set forth to investigate Mynwy-town. Agincourt Square is the sort of small-scale, intimate place you might expect to find in the middle of a small French town – Agincourt, for example – although this one is of course named after the battle won in 1415 by Henry V, who was born at Monmouth Castle and whose white statue adorns the façade of the square's Market Hall. Of more interest to me, though, was the grey statue in front of it.

It celebrates a splendid chap named Charles who, though born in London in 1877, came from a local Monmouthshire family. His father being Baron Llangattock, Charles was educated at Eton and Cambridge. In 1895 he was the owner of the third car in all Wales; in 1903 he was the second Briton to be licensed to fly by the Royal Aero Club; was there a 'first' on the horizon for young Charles? Alas, there was. In 1910, at just 33, he became the first Briton to be killed in an air accident, while flying at Bournemouth. The reason he is commemorated so proudly that the statue of a mere king skulks in the background is that in 1906 Charles got together with his friend Henry to set up a rather successful vehicle manufacturing company that, nearly a hundred years after his death, is still a major force in aero engines and a byword for luxury not just in motor cars, but in anything. His friend was Henry Royce and this is a statue to the inimitable Charles Rolls, examining the model of an early biplane.

I wandered down to the local museum. Upstairs in a quiet corner was a splendid photograph in which even the Rolls' vast family home, The Hendre, is dwarfed by a huge balloon, in whose basket Charles had just flown his mother the four miles from Monmouth. A knot of excited well-wishers and an attentive little dog surround the newfangled machine. Great days.

Out on the main street, the busy tea-time traffic seemed rather mundane, but it was a short enough walk down to the Monnow – indeed, every walk in this tiny town is a short one. Between Monmouth and its suburb of Over Monnow, the river is spanned by an impressive thirteenth-century bridge sporting an even more impressive defensive gate, the only one in Wales still *in situ* on a bridge. Above the archway can clearly be seen the openings through which the town's guards would drop onto any would-be intruders a mixture of suitably dissuasive materials. This structure and many other historical artefacts are depicted beyond the bridge on a very original, circular information board – or rather sculpture – whose three-dimensional format had so far deterred any local graffiti vandal.

Maybe Monmouth is the only town in the country without such vandals. Certainly, I couldn't imagine the pupils of its two most prestigious schools defacing their town. Strolling across a breezy riverside meadow, I re-emerged next to the impressive building out of which the boys had earlier been spilling: Monmouth School, founded, according to a handy plaque, by the Worshipful Company of Haberdashers. The girls had been escaping from the nearby Haberdashers' Monmouth School for Girls. These haberdashers had evidently got the local education scene sewn up.

My circuit of the town had brought me back to Agincourt Square, where the gathering dusk allowed the lights from two inns to tempt the weary traveller. After just four miles in the saddle I hardly qualified, but still couldn't resist. The first served up a pint of The Rev. James, quite strong and fruity, the second a rather more bland offering from the local Kingstone Brewery. The fact, however, that the latter was pulled by a young woman singing to herself convinced me to eat here, opting for the 'Welsh Chilli'. I think it was the beef rather than the chilli beans that were locally sourced.

This pub was one of the splendid J. D. Wetherspoon chain and thus boasted a fine display of local old photographs, my favourite of which showed a 1922 sheep sale down by the Monnow Bridge, where everyone present wore an almost identical cloth cap – except some of the sheep, of course. A good number of Wetherspoon's pubs also place well-stocked bookshelves behind the tables and in this case, as I sat down to my chilli, I was able to pull out a battered history book covering Europe from 1789 to 1939. I turned to the index in search of 'Wales'. Nothing. In that turbulent period, apparently nothing at all happened here. Lucky old Wales.

Day 2

The Valley of Death: Monmouth to Hay-on-Wye

It had rained overnight, but the puddles of Agincourt Square sparkled up at a blue sky as I walked across to the newsagent's. Over a poached egg I compared the opinions of the national and local weather forecasters. They agreed: strong westerlies over Wales today. (If they printed the same every day of the year, they'd surely be right more than half the time.) My route being essentially northwards, this didn't sound too bad.

Munching some buttered toast, I checked the rest of the *Monmouthshire Beacon* (established 1837) to see what hot topics currently gripped this eastern corner of the principality. A number of greater-crested newts had been transferred to a new pond in Usk (front-page headline); a Chepstow man had been arrested after forty-six cannabis plants were discovered in tents in his bedroom; and the annual Llangattock-Vibon-Avel hedging and wire-fencing match had seen the all-comers hedging title go to a stocky chap from Llanvihangel Crucorney, pictured gleaming with mud and pride. As evidence for the 'still a strange land' theory, the *Monmouthshire Beacon* was pocketed carefully in my big blue bag.

The morning's route took me whizzing down to and over Monnow Bridge, where black-blazered schoolboys balanced recklessly on the parapet – an undisputable detention offence in my day, but perhaps nowadays the journey to school is out of the headmaster's jurisdiction. On one particularly scorching afternoon in the early 1960s, a fellow Grammar School pupil of mine was put in detention simply for having been spotted capless while riding on a bus.

Metropolitan Monmouth soon gave way to a tight network of country lanes crawling over the low hills to the west of the Monnow. Heavy droplets from the night's rain still glistened in the grass verges, while the frequent gaps in roadside hedgerows revealed deep-green meadows with corners of rather muddy sheep and the occasional tiny, pure-white lamb. Though never severe, the slopes of these first few miles rose and fell like the easy swell of a great green lake. As I slowly creaked along the B-road, a lady dog-walker held her charge close against the hedge to let me past, giving me the opportunity to try out three words of Welsh – about thirty per cent of my entire vocabulary.

'*Bore da. Diolch.*' (Good morning. Thanks.)

'S'alright.'

At least she understood.

Just short of the village of Rockfield, behind a sign warning of 'Video Surveillance', a cluster of buildings in the trees hid a surprising history. These were Rockfield Studios, the world's first residential recording studio, that is to say one where the artists can stay overnight while recording... or rather, if I understand correctly the typical rock musician's schedule, 'overday'. It was here in 1975 that Queen laid down the track that was to spend fourteen weeks as the UK's No.1: 'Bohemian Rhapsody'. Any way the wind blew didn't apparently matter to Freddie Mercury. If Freddie was a cyclist, he was a fitter one than me.

The freshening westerly didn't matter too much as I dipped in and out of tiny valleys along ever narrower lanes until reaching the hamlet of Llangattock-Vibon-Avel, not only the venue for the previous week's famous hedging championship but also, about a hundred years before, the last resting place for the Welsh half of Rolls-Royce. It was in search of this that I rattled down a steep muddy path and over a half-rotten cattle grid to the tiny parish church that lies a mile from the family home, now a golf clubhouse. The Rolls headstones were immediately obvious as the largest in the graveyard, standing in a neat row overlooked by a child's home-made swing, which swayed in the wind from a sturdy branch in the garden next door. Charles Rolls lies between his parents and his elder brother, who died in World War

One. It was difficult to imagine a greater contrast between the roar of the engines that he helped create and this peaceful scene in rural Wales.

'Gattock' is an anglicisation of Catwg, the local saint, making 'Llangattock' the sacred place of Catwg, but there the explanation ends: not even the *Encyclopaedia of Wales* seems to know what the 'Vibon-Avel' means.

My next objective lay about five miles due west and so the wind did now slow my progress as I pushed the bike up every up-slope and walked it down a good number of the down-slopes, whose muddy surfaces and sharp bends argued against saddling up. Walking pace had its compensation, though, as a tame blackbird bounced along beside me and below the bare hedgerows the late-winter trinity of snowdrops, primroses and daffodils, the latter waving wildly, competed for admiration.

The longest and toughest uphill push took me right to my target: White Castle. This part of the route passed through the heart of the Welsh Marches, the traditional border zone. As the Norman invasion of Britain proceeded westward in the eleventh and twelfth centuries (Phase 5 in the Simple History), the Marches were to prove a particular source of trouble. (Well, Norman, it's you that started it.) So the invaders created a series of Marcher lordships, theoretically part of Wales but in practice partly independent of both Wales and England, having power to hold courts, build castles, wage war, etc. Oddly, a map of Wales in 1300 would show that the Marches actually occupied more land than the rest of Wales itself. The particular territory over which today's route would pass formed at one time the lordships of Monmouth and Ewyas and at another included the lordship of the Three Castles. White Castle dates from the twelfth century or possibly earlier and, together with Grosmont and Skenfrith, formed a strategic triangle of castles controlling this part of the southern Marches. The Marcher lordships were abolished in 1536 as part of Wales's union with (or annexation by) England – effectively uniting these eastern lands with the rest of Wales, from which they had been quite distinct.

White Castle was free to enter and completely deserted. Leaning the bike against an information board, I scrambled up one of the narrow spiral staircases, where my helmet provided protection against the rough-worn stonework. The name 'White' derives from the colour of the early rendering, now almost entirely worn off. From the panoramic view at the top, looking over the Trothy Valley to the west and towards the Monnow Valley in the east, it was easy to see how this fortification must have completely dominated the landscape for centuries. With its impressive moat, still partly filled, it was difficult to imagine how anyone could ever have taken it.

By the time I regained the entrance, two workers had come back from a break in their Cardiff-registered van and resumed their thorough painting of the site's railings. Aware of the castle's history, one of them offered me a 600-year guarantee on their work.

A welcome downhill spurt took me through my second Llangattock of the day, on to my first Llanfihangel and opened up views of the first Black Mountains of the trip.

Recently discovered documents include the minutes of the ancient Welsh Geographical Naming Committee, a translated extract from which reads...

> Williams Chairman: 'Right, boyos, we've got another mountain to name. Any suggestions?'
> Williams Creative: 'What about White Mountain?'
> Williams Pedantic: 'It's not white.'
> Williams Creative: 'All right, Green Mountain then.'
> Williams Queasy: 'Green makes me sick.'
> Williams Chairman: 'There's always Black Mountain.'
> Williams Creative: 'There are already twelve Black Mountains in Wales.'
> Williams Chairman: 'So?'
> Silence.
> Williams Chairman: 'Black Mountain it is then. Now, what about these three new villages? Is Llanfihangel OK for all of them?'

Actually, according to the Ordnance Survey's *Gazetteer*, Wales has about 220 Llan-somethings, including seventeen Llanfihangels or Llanvihangels, from the Welsh Mihangel (St Michael). At one point you clearly couldn't move in Wales without stepping in someone's sacred place. There are, in truth, only three Black Mountains.

Regretting my lack of training for this ride, at Llanvihangel Crucorney I pulled to a thankful halt at Wales's oldest pub (it says outside): the Skirrid Mountain Inn. The amiable

English landlord took one look at the pale, wind-blown cyclist and recommended a lunch of hot soup and coffee. Concurring, I slumped into a chair and reviewed the map. I'd done about eighteen miles, just over halfway through the day by distance, but the afternoon looked like it would be a bleak one.

To put this, and the route as a whole, into context, I needed a geographical equivalent to the Absurdly Simple History of Wales. (Geographers, look away now.)

An Absurdly Simple Geography of Wales

Wales is essentially a lump of hills, drained by rivers in all directions. The most extensive range is the Cambrian Mountains, creating a watershed aligned north–south, with Snowdonia appended to the north and a number of outliers to the south, including the Brecon Beacons, the Black Mountains and, er, Black Mountain. Those rivers that drain the eastern slopes have the longest journey to the sea – notably the Dee, Severn, Wye and Usk – some of which flow into England, while those draining the northern, western and southern slopes are shorter but often dramatic. Apart from the river valleys, the only other extensive lowlands lie near the coast, notably Anglesey, Pembrokeshire and the Vale of Glamorgan. The dominance of Wales's highlands, typical of Britain's western fringes, has acted both as a defence against outside influences and as a barrier to communications and development.

In aiming at three extreme coastal locations, my route would cross and re-cross these hills. I hoped machine and rider would both be up to the job. The afternoon's task was to cross the Black Mountains via an unnumbered road that snakes north up the glaciated valley of the River Honddu, over Gospel Pass and down into Hay-on-Wye, where overnight accommodation was reserved and where the other half of the team should be waiting.

On a previous long-distance bike ride in Scotland (which you can read about in my first book, *From the Mull to the Cape*, Summersdale 2008) I'd discovered that my weak knees and my penchant for carrying too much equipment were incompatible. The solution hatched there was to be adopted here in Wales too: my infinitely patient and improbably talented partner Julie would form a one-woman support team and mobile equipment store. For most of the journey, while I pedalled at snail's pace between overnight stops, Julie would apply her map-reading skills to zigzagging along a parallel route in the golden Toyota Yaris, apply her shopping skills to sniffing out local bargains and use her culinary experience to identify the best place to eat each evening. Our overnight stops would usually be booked a couple of nights in advance and, except for in Monmouth, which I did alone, another of Julie's tasks would be to arrive there first and, if necessary, guide me to our accommodation by mobile phone. If only Livingstone had been lucky enough to have had this support. With such back-up, crossing the Black Mountains should be easy-peasy, shouldn't it?

Duly souped up and cartographically informed, I was looking around at my fellow diners when a disagreement between two of them led to one standing up and asking us all:

'Excuse me, does anyone know what day it is?'

One Monday and two Tuesdays were offered, leaving the aggregate score 2–3 until the landlord stated with a suitable air of authority:

'It's Tuesday.'

How far from civilisation had I already ventured? I paid up but, before I left the landlord invited me to take a look at his noose. And indeed, just a few steps behind the bar, hanging from an old beam in the well of the staircase was a sturdy rope ending in an ominous noose. It's reputed that from around the year 1110 a court was held right here at the Skirrid Inn, a local sheep-stealer being the first of about 180 villains to be hanged from the inn's beam, some having been sentenced by the infamous 'Hanging' Judge Jeffreys, sent from London to sort things out. In fact, the despatch of hard men from London to deal with the troublesome Welsh seems to have been an occurrence repeated through history. Saddling up again outside the inn, I felt that I'd temporarily slipped not only some way from civilisation, but some time back from it too.

The start of the route up the Honddu Valley, also known as the Vale of Ewyas, was a surprising downhill, under the Hereford–Abergavenny railway line and pleasantly alongside the river. Little blue-and-red Sustrans signs declared this as Route 42 on the National Cycle Network (NCN 42), an encouraging hint that other people had actually cycled along there.

After a mile or two, the gradients had steepened and I soon dismounted for a slug of cold water and a stare across the valley at the misshapen Cwmyoy church, pulled this way and that by land movement. As the road turned north I'd expected the mass of hills on the left to shelter me from the west wind, but quite the opposite happened: the wind strengthened, coming straight at me from the north, turning bitterly cold to boot. At the next breathless water stop I glared accusingly up at the sky where little cloudlets danced gaily to the forecasters' tune, west to east, while down here in the valley bottom the weather system seemed to be operating at right angles. By the time I'd slumped against the crumbling walls of Llanthony Priory, I was trying to phone Julie to warn of my likely late arrival in Hay... but there was no mobile signal. Taking comfort in a Skirrid-sourced sandwich, I wandered around the ruins of the priory.

The story goes that during a storm a Norman knight, William de Lacy, was so impressed by the shelter offered by a chapel hereabouts that he converted to Christianity on the spot. Believe that if you like, but what definitely did happen was that the followers who joined him founded an Augustinian priory here in the twelfth century and that the delicate ruins among which I was now munching my sandwich are what remains of a building from about 1180. Following the damage from various English attacks and Welsh rebellions, Llanthony Priory was closed as part of Henry VIII's dissolution of the monasteries in 1538.

This distraction had revived me a little and, before pushing on, to give me something else to think about than a cold face and an aching back, I took a glance at some notes made before starting the journey. They told me that the peak to the west, so conspicuously failing to give me shelter, was Pen y Gadair Fawr, and at 800 metres it is the highest point at this latitude between Saskatoon in Canada and Novosibirsk in Siberia. I drew no encouragement from this.

Beyond the priory the road narrowed still further and wandered three-dimensionally between hedges or trees, hiding from view all but the weedy carriageway itself. Even when the gradient didn't make me dismount, the etiquette of letting motor vehicles past did. Just before Capel-y-ffin, my map – but no road sign – told me that I was finally leaving Monmouthshire and entering old Breconshire in the modern county of Powys. Breconshire got its name from the fifth-century kingdom of Brycheiniog, which was reputedly – and that far back in Wales pretty much everything seems to be merely 'reputed' – named after its ruler Brychan, whose very existence is only reputed. Powys definitely did exist, as one of the ancient Welsh kingdoms, the name coming (reputedly) from the Latin *pagus*, meaning countryside. Powys re-emerged in the 1974 changes, survived the 1996 hatchet-job and is now the largest county in Wales.

Just round the corner another leftover from ancient times appeared and, dumping the bike on the verge, I dived straight into it: a snug and warm, bright and red BT telephone box. Having found forty pence (a quadrupling in price since my last usage) and called Julie to let her know that I was running – or rather plodding – late, I gobbled up my last Skirrid sandwich while being closely observed by a bemused young spaniel who had clearly never before seen a human in 'his' phone box.

With the route settling into a steady uphill, and the headwind unrelenting, the Fourth Law of Cycle Touring came into full play:

Wind and gradient are effectively the same thing.

(A thousand miles in the saddle through Scotland and Wales have prompted the conception of ten such 'laws', most probably familiar to every touring cyclist and all listed at the end of this book.) From here to the top it would be all push and no ride. With my chin virtually touching the big, blue handlebar bag, I wondered if any of its contents hadn't really been necessary. The smart clothes for an evening in Monmouth? The pair of sensible shoes? The hairbrush? The *Monmouthshire Beacon*? You're right: all of them. Every damned ounce of them.

A youth hostel came and went, the last stand of trees came and went, and there above the tree line lay a hint of a world beyond this infernal valley: the road disappearing over a summit. *The* summit, perhaps? Picking up my pace from snail to super-snail, I gradually approached the hilltop. Having tiptoed across a cattle grid, I stared in despair at the road ahead: across a bare, unfenced wasteland, another mile to another summit.

It was now getting distinctly dark, the last two cars having had their lights on, and so I looked for some shelter in which to don my fluorescent shoulder strap. There was none and what followed was five minutes of pure Chaplin. In the fierce wind, the strap wanted to assume only one orientation: horizontal. Several times I got it over my head, but cold fingers and flapping strap conspired to defeat any further fixture, so that eventually I just forced the loose end into my pocket and zipped it in. Having checked the mobile again (still no signal) and glugged more water (the last), I pushed once more into the gale, which was now rushing across the high moorland and thus even fiercer and even colder. The next twenty minutes are a blank, except for the vague memory of a gust so mighty that I simply crouched motionless with the bike as my shield until it abated.

The first thing that told me I'd reached the top was a sudden flow of warmth, like a hot flannel across my face. Raising my head, I was astonished to see that, beyond this Valley of Death, where the light had been rapidly fading, the sun was still up and bathed the Vale of the River Wye beyond in a golden evening light. The wind, no longer funnelled between the hills, had calmed down and I sat on a sun-kissed tuft of grass to check my mobile, welcome the signal and call Julie with the news that I was still alive. Only then did I look back into the gloom. To the east loomed Hay Bluff and to the west Lord Hereford's Knob, with no sign of his lordship attached. Here in the middle was Gospel Pass, named after a twelfth-century tour of these parts by the Archbishop of Canterbury and his preacher, Gerald of Wales, to recruit soldiers for the controversial invasion of a Middle Eastern country. That was the Third Crusade but it sounded vaguely familiar.

With not many minutes to sunset and with my larder empty, I wasted no more time before assuming the uncommon position of cyclist aboard cycle to push off downhill. It was an exhilarating – though even colder – descent, demanding

38

all my concentration not just for cycling but also for 'psychling', defined as the mental emission of 'Get out of the way' beams to all sheep, geese, dogs and Land Rovers loitering in the way of a bicycle in top gear.

After five miles in just twenty minutes, I was relieved finally to pull up in the pub car park, where the five-foot-nothing form of Julie skipped up to hug me and pepper me with questions, to which I could respond only in rasping grunts. Five minutes later she was insisting that, before I inflict a hot shower on my ice-blue toes, they would benefit from the attention of radiator-warmed socks. Bliss indeed! I wondered how much they'd charge for this in Soho.

Down in the bar and halfway down a bottle of wine, I was eventually able to utter a few words and the first were 'cottage' and 'pie'.

'Same for me,' said Julie, 'and the dessert board looks good too.'

As usual, she'd taken in our surroundings more quickly and comprehensively than I had. In fact, Julie would give a much more accurate description of the views from the bike saddle too, but, though an occasional cyclist, she draws the line not only at cycling uphill, but also at cycling downhill and cycling in the wet. Oh, and cycling in traffic. This seems to leave just Holland on a dry day – which indeed we've done. Journeys by almost any other means, though, she's always up for and seemed happy with her current role as zigzagging support driver. After she'd dropped me at Symonds Yat she'd popped over to Gloucestershire to stay with her parents and then wound her way back through Herefordshire to Hay.

'Pretty calm in England,' she remarked, 'and here too. Where was this wind you're on about?'

'In the Valley of Death. I told you.'

'That's not even its name. Stop exaggerating.'

'The wind must have been following me then.'

'Sounds familiar,' her eyes rolled and settled on something behind me. 'What on Earth's going on over there?'

Although I hadn't noticed from my position slumped in a chair, the bar had already begun to fill up when a surreal country-and-western version of 'Amazing Grace' announced the beginning of 'Open Mike Night'. I'm still not sure that what followed wasn't a waking nightmare – it sounded like a cat was being forced to scrape its claws down a blackboard in front of the microphone. However, Julie, who could actually see what was going on, assured me that no animal was involved other than a man with a fiddle. He interrupted himself to say that he'd never done this in public before and then continued to prove that he'd never done it in private either. After he'd put the tortured instrument down, the embarrassed smirks of the audience turned to wide-eyed horror when the Scraper, instead of slinking off to self-imposed exile in remotest Peru, started to sing an unaccompanied ballad. I say 'sing', but 'murder' would be more accurate; I say 'ballad' but no one had any idea what it was supposed to be. Some people looked away, others looked into their beer, yet others simply walked out and were heard guffawing outside. The guffawing was considerably more tuneful than whatever it was that the Scraper was doing. The English landlady came over to assure us that 'Open Mike Nights' usually served up better fare.

At last he came to the end of the song and was encouraged to return to his seat, apparently – and this is perhaps the most remarkable aspect of the affair – still sober. More regular open-mikers took his place and committed more tuneful murders of a few Dylan classics before we creaked upstairs to an early slumber.

Day 3

The Painscastle Pact:
Hay-on-Wye to
Llandrindod Wells

After a solid ten hours I awoke listless. The previous day had taken it out of me and now I knew what it had taken out: *list*, meaning 'appetite' in Middle English. Fortunately, I'd scheduled today's to be a shorter ride, to allow for a morning's trundle around Hay, and so I pulled my limp limbs into some kind of order to accompany Julie out into the street. Our nostrils were accosted by a strange smell, which she identified as coming from the kind of wood they habitually burn in India. Maybe they were burning last night's Scraper.

In fact, Hay-on-Wye looked rather French: that's two towns out of two so far. The pub where we were staying was adorned by a jolly veranda where espresso and pastis wouldn't look out of place – in the right weather. The tiny twisting streets of the town centre, through which Inspector Clouseau's vehicle could have hurtled at any moment, lay squeezed between the River Wye and a seventeenth-century manor house that occupies the site of the old castle.

I can remember this little market town from the 1950s. On family visits to stay with the resident engineer at the Pontsticill Reservoir near Merthyr – better known to me as Uncle Cyril – Hay-on-Wye is where our light-blue Morris Minor (registration FDB 932) crossed the border into Wales. As soon as we were parked up, I'd clamber out of the back seat onto a foreign pavement, look at foreign signs, drink foreign lemonade and, if I was lucky, hear someone speak in a foreign language. I wish I'd asked Auntie Kitty to teach it to me, but it seemed to me literally incredible that anyone could actually communicate in these words without laughing. The same applied, of course, to French, German or any language other than English.

Nowadays, according to travel guides, Hay's full name is Haysecondhandbookcapitaloftheworld-on-Wye. It was in 1965 that Richard Booth turned up to start the second-hand book business which, rumour had it, dominates the place to the extent that you can't find any ordinary businesses for the locals. Happily, this proved untrue.

There are, admittedly, some forty-five bookshops and we browsed through a few, including Booth's own Hay Castle Bookshop. Having resisted the rack full of old family photos (in case you don't have a family of your own?), I sniffed around for the cheaper books. The latest category of book to fall on hard times at the very bottom of the bargain basement seemed to be social science hardbacks. For thirty pence you could learn all you ever wanted to know about 'Organisational Behaviour in the Modern World', where 'modern' is the 1960s. For a mere twenty pence you could pore over the 'Reasons for Rural De-Population in Mid-Wales'. When I spotted one of the texts that had bolstered much of my own first-year social science studies, I retreated back up into twenty-first-century daylight.

The wind had died down, my *list* had returned and the swish of the tarmac called. Having happily ejected from my heavy blue bag all that unnecessary rubbish and replaced it with a more useful tube of Deep Heat, I agreed where to meet Julie in Llandrindod Wells that evening and cruised off in confidence, turning right at the main road. Three minutes later I retraced my route and turned left instead.

The old man who'd put me on the right track told me to follow 'the road to Cairo', which turned out to be the road to Clyro, a tiny village just across the river. The Wye here seemed broader than downstream at Monmouth, an odd phenomenon. As I crossed I looked out for the line of Offa's Dyke. The dyke and the border wander from south to north like two ribbons flapping in the wind, one minute stuck together, the next blown apart. The previous afternoon, while I'd been struggling up the Valley of Death, the lines of the dyke and the border had been marching in tandem along the top of the ridge to the east, and from Hay Bluff they dance apart en route to the Wye at Hay. Here they rejoin, the river acting as both for a while, until Offa's defence becomes a dyke again a mile or so to the north.

Offa was the king of Mercia, a powerful kingdom enlarged from its original base in the modern-day West Midlands. This was in Phase 4 (the 'small, squabbling kingdom' phase in the Simple History) and it was during the eighth century that Offa embarked on what was at the time the biggest engineering project in Europe: the creation of a dyke and ditch along his western frontier, to hinder incursions from Powys and other Welsh kingdoms. The footpath that now follows the line of the dyke was opened in 1971 and is 177 miles from end to end.

From here the dyke, the path and border all shoot off northwards towards Hergest Ridge, a hill with two tales to tell. It was the legendary home of the Black Dog of Hergest, believed by some to have been the inspiration behind *The Hound of the Baskervilles*, as Conan Doyle wrote the story shortly after staying at nearby Hergest Hall. Many years later Mike Oldfield named his 1974 follow-up to *Tubular Bells* after Hergest Ridge, because he could see it from the house that was his bolt-hole from all the hoo-ha that followed his sudden rise to fame.

Having crossed the Wye, however, I pedalled north-west into old Radnorshire. The county's Welsh name is Maesyfed, *maes* meaning 'open field' and seen more often nowadays in *maes parcio*: car park. Maesyfed means the territory of

Hyfaidd, another of those early Welsh chieftains. The English name comes from the original county town of Radnor, some way to the east and even smaller as an old county town than Monmouth.

From Clyro the ground rose steadily, giving intermittent views back south to the Black Mountains and the Brecon Beacons. I huffed past the edge of The Begwns, a hilltop common owned by the National Trust; skimmed down into the scenic valley of the little Bachawy and puffed up the other side again into the small village of Painscastle, whose twelfth-century castle was named after, yes, a chap called Pain: Pain Fitz John, in fact. His parents evidently knew even before his christening what kind of child he would be.

The short, six-mile hop from Hay had taken me one and a half hours. Four miles per hour. Time, as Lionel Bart's Fagin said, to review the situation. I slumped into a convenient bus stop and poured some coffee from the flask. Spitting it out, my first decision was to vow never again to make a flask from a hotel's complimentary coffee tray. It's always orange and this stuff looked and tasted positively radioactive. Next was my route. Perhaps my question at the start of the ride should have been less 'Why am I doing this?' than 'How am I going to manage it?' I was trying to stick reasonably close to my straight, kitchen-pencil line between Monmouth and Anglesey, hence all the ups and downs. For whatever reason – age, weight, unfitness, wind (not mine): a list to be analysed more calmly later – this was proving problematic. I looked closely at the contours and the contours looked closely back at me. We agreed to try and avoid each other for the time being and together we eschewed the potential delights of

Cregrina, the hilly outpost where the *Encyclopaedia* had excelled itself in uncovering a rumour that Wales's last wolf was killed here in the 1500s (how would anyone have known it was the last?) Instead we favoured a flatter, though longer, route down to the main road and up the Wye Valley to Builth Wells and beyond. The Wye seemed to be drawing me ever back like a fluvial magnet.

Adopting a psychological device I'd used before, I gave my little agreement with the contours a name – the Painscastle Pact – the better to remember and adhere to it. Within half a mile I knew this was the right move, for the B4594 from Painscastle to Erwood is surely one of the most scenic and, judging from the lack of traffic, one of the most secret touring routes in Wales. Soft sunshine glittered on the Bachawy, blackbirds sang from proud stands of hillside trees, sheep munched away contentedly in the riverside meadows and some watched over a few tiny white lambs. Today's wayside daffodils were calmer, not bobbing their heads in the wind but glancing coyly at their neighbours to see if they'd soon join them in the daylight. I even managed more than a few hundred yards without dismounting. This was more like it.

I'd brought Ordnance Survey maps of two scales: the 1:175,000 Travel Series and the 1:50,000 Landranger Series. On a ride of similar length in Western Scotland, where features are large, turnings rare and roads consistent in orientation, the smaller scale had proved ideal. Here in Mid-Wales, however, where the topography is more low-key and the road network denser, I was finding the 1:50,000 more useful, although changing sheets was more frequent, of course. My failure to change to the next sheet while lazily trolling along the B4594 was why the road's sudden, dramatic descent into the valley at Erwood took me and my brakes by surprise. We juddered and squeaked round several hairpins before emerging once again on a bridge over the Wye... and once again the river seemed even broader upstream than down.

Two parallel roads, one either side of the river, covered the seven miles from here to Builth Wells. The Painscastle Pact came into play again, directing me to the west bank and the gentler gradient of the A470, which wasn't too busy at this time of year. It must be rare for a road to have its own entry in an encyclopaedia, especially by its modern road number, but the *Encyclopaedia of Wales* strikes another blow for originality and identifies the A470 as emblematic of the country's unity by running all the way from Cardiff to Llandudno... except that perhaps it doesn't. According to my OS map it takes a break between Llangurig and Llanidloes. As this stretch was on my intended route, I made a note to check it out. Surely the *Encyclopaedia* couldn't have made a mistake on page one!

According to a mountain bike website (www.mtb-marathon. co.uk), Builth Wells is 'the unofficial capital of the UK mountain bike marathon scene'. Every town around here seems to be the unofficial capital of something or other. I knew that Llanwrtyd Wells, a few miles to the west but off my route, is the unofficial capital of men running against horses and other men (or, more worryingly, the same men) snorkelling through bogs. More exhibits for the 'strange land' evidence bag, I think. At the time I visited it, the mountain bike website went on to announce a forthcoming cycling event in the hills around Builth. Nothing strange about that... except that this race would take place *in the middle of the night*. See what I mean?

This cyclist was of an altogether different species, with different priorities. On arrival in Builth I spied a friendly looking cafe and sat down to tea and buttered scones, with a dash of strawberry jam to celebrate the signing of the Painscastle Pact. A glance at the map showed me why Builth is here, surveying the lowlands of the Ithon and Upper Wye Valleys, guarding access to the southern highlands and to the Lower Wye Valley which pierces them. With a river crossing point too, it was clear that the ever-strategic Normans would plant a town here and slap one of their standard castles above it. They did both. The 'Wells' suffix derives, as with Llanwrtyd and Llandrindod, from the Victorian passion for 'taking the waters'. The waters they took in Builth were saline waters from one well and sulphur waters from another and, Victorians being as predictable as Normans, a railway helped them get here and a flurry of cafes and hotels sprang up to entertain them when the thrill of the waters had worn off. The decline of the spa trade has been partly offset by the presence just across the river of the Royal Welsh Showground, with its new and splendidly exotic towers. Its posters revealed the variety of uses to which this venue is being put: within a few weeks it was due to host an antiques fair, two dog shows, one stallion show, a 'green' buildings exhibition and a meeting of the Welsh Beekeepers Association.

With dinner in the company of old friends on my mind, I soon buzzed off myself. The sign at the bridge announced seven miles to Llandrindod Wells and then about a mile later another declared that it was still seven miles. Doesn't that kind of thing annoy you? It was an undulating route around the corner of the Wye and Ithon Valleys and going-home time meant that each motor that edged past me was followed closely by another. Wondering why it was that posh German makes – BMW, Mercedes and especially Audi – always travel so close to me and to each other, I put my head down and pressed on.

The road rose steadily at first, between dark stands of conifers that hid Llanelwedd Quarry, from where the stone for many of Builth's buildings originated. As the route flattened out, a track to the left led to an elegant, pink mansion. Now a hotel, this artfully placed, eighteenth-century building was once the home of landscape artist Thomas Jones, for whom the views must have been a factor drawing him back from a lengthy European tour. With my own eyes often fixed on the rear wheels of a truck or the bumper of a four-by-four, this main-road stretch from Erwood, where the Painscastle B-road had emerged, to Llandrindod Wells, offered only occasional glances at the patchwork of fields stretching east to Radnor Forest or west to the much higher and darker Cambrian Mountains.

Eventually the hilly route I'd intended to take, via the last wolf's last resting place, came swooping in at Howey and I was soon sitting up in the saddle to take in the grand architecture of downtown Llandrindod Wells – or, as the locals understandably call it, Llan'dod.

Llan'dod is the perfect British seaside town – except that the sea is about thirty-five miles away. The seaside atmosphere is, of course, once again down to those Victorians and their waters. Unlike Builth, however, Llan'dod still pumps the theme for all its worth, putting on a popular 'Victorian Week' every August, which recalls as best it can the thriving nineteenth-century scene. Certainly, the architecture still fits the bill, with plenty of very grand and, even nowadays, very smart-looking Victorian terraces. It also looked like the largest hotel, the magnificent Metropole, had recently had a makeover. Even the railway station looked the part, but for me its delights would have to await the next day, as I hurried to our accommodation: not the Metropole, but a humbler sixteenth-century inn. Its sign promised a 'Sixteenth-century Welcome'. As I pulled up by the door, a broad man in a fringed Western jacket and cowboy boots approached.

'Howdy there!' he called.

Sixteenth-century Welsh, nineteenth-century American... whatever.

One oddity about Wales that is certainly true is the profusion of a relatively small number of surnames: Jones, Davies, Williams, Owen... and not many more. This arises from the imposition of the Teutonic English system, whereby everyone has to have a surname. In the traditional Celtic system, children were known simply by their father's name: e.g. Owain ap Rhys (Owen, son of Rhys). So 'son of Rhys' eventually became Price, son of John became Jones, son of David became Davies or Davis, and so on. From this developed the strategy of adding an unofficial suffix to distinguish, say, one David Owen from another: David Owen Coal as opposed to David Owen Foreign Secretary.

This explains my unusual response when my old university friend Rhodri greeted me in the bar of our hotel.

'Richard, you're a bit greyer but still the same old you.'

'Davies Sanitary, you're a bit wider but till the same old you too!'

Many years ago I happened to be with Rhodri when he called in at a local South Wales shoe-repairer's to collect a pair of his father's shoes. Many, if not most, of the shoes on the shelf bore the name Davies. After a brief description of the Davies in question, the assistant said:

'Oh, you mean Davies Sanitary!'

Rhodri's father was the local public health inspector.

After Julie and Rhodri's friend Jane had joined us, drinks were in place and food on order, I asked Rhodri if these Welsh nicknames were dying out.

'Oh, far from it,' he said. 'When we got the first traffic warden in our town, it was yet another Dai, unfortunately. To distinguish him from all the others employed by the local authority, this one was instantly re-christened "Dai Book and Pencil".'

'My favourite one,' I offered, 'is the tale of the Russian agent. He was on a secret assignment to meet a Mr Jones in a certain village in the Valleys. He presents himself at the local pub, asking the landlord for Mr Jones. "Well," says the landlord. "There's quite a few 'ere. Where are you from, sir?" "From, er, from Eastern Europe." "Oh, you'll want Jones Spy – he's sittin' over there."'

It's odd, but whatever serious twists and turns our various lives have taken, whenever I meet up with old chums from university, the common currency soon reverts to jokes.

'Sometimes the best jokes are from real life,' suggested Rhodri, 'especially when you work for local government.'

Jane seconded this with gusto. Both she and Rhodri had spent years experiencing the unique cocktail of pain and pleasure that seemed to come from working closely with Powys County Council.

'Their latest idea is to get us all out of our cars and into buses,' said Rhodri. 'A great idea in theory, but... well... how long do you think I've lived at my current address, Richard?'

'Oh, thirty years, surely.'

'More or less. And do you think I might be aware of the local bus services? And might have considered them as a way of getting to the office?'

'Almost certainly.'

'Well, the council seems to think it may not have occurred to me and so they sent me – and hundreds of others – an expensively produced glossy brochure telling me exactly which buses – yes, buses plural – could get me from home to work in about an hour and a half, including a stiff walk that actually retraces the route already taken by one of these buses!'

'How long does it take you to drive there?' asked Julie.

'Ten minutes at most.'

We all laughed. Outside of work, Rhodri's passion is singing; more specifically, singing in a cathedral choir; more specifically still, travelling with the choir all over Europe, where his four or five languages must make him all but indispensable.

'Odd things are afoot in the cathedral too,' he revealed, supping another pint of Hancock's. 'We recently appointed a new organist – but of course the new man, an excellent individual of many talents, was far too busy to actually play the organ.'

I spluttered on my own beer. I love these little true tales of absurdity and Rhodri is a master at storing them up and – dare I say it? – even enhancing them.

'So what do you think we did?'

'Chained him to the organ?' suggested Julie.

'Ha!' laughed Jane. 'It's even sillier. Listen.'

'Well,' continued Rhodri. 'We advertised another vacancy to be filled, because the cathedral also needs an organ-playing organist...'

More splutters.

'Only in Wales, surely,' I suggested, but Rhodri revealed that this arrangement is not uncommon in cathedral circles.

Well fed and well entertained, we said our goodbyes – but happily in the knowledge that we'd meet Rhodri again later in this trip.

Day 4

Riots and Rebellions: Llandrindod Wells to Llanidloes

'Morning. Quite a tremor!' said our landlord, when we came down for breakfast. Our blank looks prompted more. 'The earthquake. Five-point-two on the... er... the...'

'Richter scale?' offered Julie.

'That's the one. Biggest for twenty-five years, they say.'

The merry meal and our usual heavy sleeping must have been why neither Julie nor I had felt anything at all.

'Where?' I asked.

'Lincolnshire somewhere. Re-arranged some of the pictures on our walls, mind.'

'Bit difficult to tell,' I offered, having noticed their odd angles last night.

'Ah, fair comment. Is it tea or coffee then?'

With a short day of only about twenty-five miles ahead, breakfast was leisurely and we had time to take in the charms of Llan'dod, a town that seems to be all centre and no suburbs. The first was the little, though important, railway station. With around 5,000 inhabitants, Llandrindod Wells is not only the biggest place for miles around but also the home of Powys County Council, and so supplies a fair chunk of passengers for the 'Heart of Wales' line, one of only two passenger lines to cross Mid-Wales and in a constant battle for survival.

From the platform a handwritten notice for a book sale attracted us into the ticket office, where several old photos of the station were on display, many depicting a remarkably fresh-faced Elizabeth Windsor showing Llan'dod the latest 1950s fashions. As the stationmaster had no customers, I asked him through the hatch when these photos were taken. Silently raising his finger, he disappeared from view only to re-emerge in the public area with finger still raised and now beckoning me to follow. Wondering if I was being led to the gallows for having enquired after personal data relating to Her Maj, I followed him out onto the platform and to the very edge of the rails, where the moving finger was lowered to point at an inscription engraved on a grey plaque on the floor. It revealed that the foot placed right there on 23 October 1952 was the first regal foot that

Elizabeth had placed in Wales after she'd become Queen. Gosh.

'I'm sorry, sir.' The stationmaster spoke for the first time. 'I just couldn't remember whether it was the twenty-third or the twenty-fifth.'

With that, he saluted and was gone. The plaque was astonishingly graffiti-free, as were all the information boards around the station, although I was a little surprised that the rail network map didn't actually include this line. The street map on display was a little odd too.

'Julie,' I said. 'Where are we?'

'Llandrindod Wells?'

'Yes, that's what I thought. This street map's of Knighton – that's sixteen miles away.'

'Well, maybe they haven't got enough streets here to put on a map,' she suggested. 'Anyway, the whole place is a bit odd. At a glance it seems like there's a lot going on, and loads of shops, but the short main street ends quite abruptly, and then that's it. On the other hand, most towns nowadays have no knitting-wool shop at all, while Llan'dod's got two.'

'Bet I can show you something stranger than that!'

'Me too!'

We set off and Julie led me to her oddity first. We walked down the main road and then up a side road to the east until we were beside a large lake.

'When I arrived yesterday,' she said, 'the hotel was closed and that cowboy bloke suggested that, if I'd got an hour to spare, I could do worse than go up to the lake to look at the ducks.'

I stared out across the lake and my eyes were met by the sight of several enormous, grey, static shapes emerging from the surface, one of which seemed to have a dragon's head, some of which may have been the rest of the beast and some others of which were probably fish. Fish doing synchronised leaping. 'He didn't mention the monster then?'

'Nope. I think it might be a dragon, actually.'

'Or the giant flying fish?'

'Nope.'

'Maybe he hasn't been up here for…'

We both tried to estimate the age of the incongruous, semi-submerged sculpture.

'… fifty years?' suggested Julie.

'OK, it's strange. But I think mine is even stranger.'

Walking back down to the town, I pulled Julie up next to the 'Tom Norton Building', a very early example of a motor showroom, begun in 1909 by local cyclist and entrepreneur Tom Norton and originally called 'The Palace of Sports'. Its art deco style includes a fascia clad in large white tiles, many of which include bold lettering in relief. I pointed Julie at the lettering.

'Who do you think the building is named after.'

'Tom Norton?' she ventured.

'Look again.'

'Oh… ah, whoops!' She read the name again exactly as it appeared in giant, old ceramic reliefs: 'TOM NOTRON.'

'Yes, it's not as though nobody's noticed – Rhodri reminded me to look out for it last night. Isn't it great they've just left that mistake in there?'

These tiny incidents had already made my day (sad, I know), but another highlight came hard on their heels, as a large part of the Tom 'Notron' Building is now taken over by the National Cycle Museum. It was much bigger than I'd expected and among the hundreds of bikes on show were shapes and sizes I'd never even thought of: four wheels, three seats, no seats, bamboo frames, leather straps... I think some of the exhibits might have been left over from the National Torture Museum. It certainly put the trivial problems with my own machine into perspective: Gears? You're lucky!

Duly chastened, I thanked the curator, asking him why the National Cycle Museum was here.

'It's got to be somewhere, sir.'

Fair play.

Julie must have been relieved when, at eleven o'clock, the tour of pompous plaques, silly ceramics and bamboo bikes was over and, having arranged to meet up in Llanidloes, I was in the saddle and waving my way up the slope to the main road. A minute later I was out of it again, replacing the chain, which tends to come off when you change down and wave at the same time. Two more minutes and I was off yet again.

The A483 northbound is soon out of Llan'dod and offering up views over the river meadows to the west. A sprinkling of snow lay on the outliers of the Cambrians, but the day was already noticeably warmer (seven degrees, the car thermometer had said), the sun was out and the cumulus billowing to the north looked to be the fair weather variety.

At breakfast I'd resisted the option taken by the guests at our neighbouring table of a small yellow mountain of scrambled egg and therefore felt reasonably confident of a comfortable day's ride as I trundled into Crossgates and pulled up at the post office.

Back in Llan'dod I'd bought a copy of *The Brecon & Radnor Express* (established 1889), whose front-page lead was 'The sad decline of rural post offices'. A common enough tale these days and the Crossgates PO that morning was a typical example: alive with the local gossip – in English and about the improving weather – and keen to supplement the dwindling post office business with all kinds of tempting snacks. In my case these were a healthy sandwich, plus a handful of Chomps for small boosts and a Boost for a big one. Don't tell the support team. I'm supposed to be watching my weight.

A mile out of Crossgates, I turned left, leaving the trucks and buses behind and immediately re-entering the quiet Mid-Wales lanes that I'd left over twenty-four hours before at Erwood. The Clywedog Brook gurgled away to my left through gentle pasture where cattle, sheep and lambs munched away, while I pedalled rhythmically up the gentle gradient into the Cambrian Mountains.

The name comes from Cambria, a Latin form of Cymru, but very few of the Cambrian 'Mountains' are actually mountains, i.e. over 2,000 feet. The word rings a louder bell in geologists' ears for the term 'Precambrian', the only other aeon on Earth than the Phanerozoic – which is the aeon in which you are reading this. The Precambrian aeon is so named because the first period in the first era in the current aeon (starting around 540 million years ago) is called the Cambrian, as Wales is where rocks from that period were first studied.

A double line of silver birch, with many more of last year's leaves than this year's, accompanied a tributary down to the brook near Bryn-Llygoed Farm, whose ornate sign pictured three happy pigs also enjoying the environment of this little valley. It seemed popular, too, with birds of prey, many of which hovered and swooped to my left, their sightings easily outnumbering those of the usual suspects – crows, magpies, blackbirds, finches, sparrows – which this morning were heard but not seen. Stopping to look more carefully at the swoopers, I was on the lookout for one whose distinctive shape I'd memorised: the red kite. Their designated feeding site at Grigin lay only a few miles to the west. The survival hereabouts of the red kite is quite a conservation success story, as this elegant bird of prey, native to what is now Wales for 125,000 years, had become almost extinct a hundred years ago. Now carefully protected, it has apparently been seen once again in every Welsh county. Not here today, though. I think mine were mostly buzzards.

Finally crossing the brook, the lane swung westwards to bring into view some higher, more distant hills. A recent national newspaper had drawn attention to the nearness of spring by showing a photograph of a field of sheep roughly forming the word 's p r i n g' and being observed by a proud sheepdog in the foreground. No doubt the careful placing of food was involved. This must have been in my mind when one hillside in the west seemed to spell out the letters 'W I' in sheep. Was this a follow-up to the Women's Institute's naked calendar?

Once again bridging the brook, the lane passed a sign announcing the village of Abbey-cwm-hir, my planned lunch stop. This was still Radnorshire and a traditional rhyme says:

> Radnorsheer, poor Radnorsheer
> Never a park, not even a deer
> Never a squire of five hundred a year
> But Richard Fowler of Abbey-cwm-hir.

This twelfth-century Cistercian monastery has been witness to more than its fair share of violence. Lending their support to the Welsh cause, the monks were persecuted by the nasty English, who fined them £200 and, for good measure, set fire to the monastery. In 1282 the Prince of Wales, Llywelyn ap Gruffudd, was buried here after being killed in a nearby battle – at least, that part of his body they could find was buried here. Then, during the fifteenth-century rebellion, Welsh hero Owain Glyndŵr destroyed most of the monastery again.

After dissolution, the land was granted to Richard Fowler (of the verse above), for his service to King Richard in the Crusades, and he had a house built here. But this was definitely not a lucky site: during the Civil War the house and any monastic remains were virtually destroyed yet again. I guess this is the gist of the rhyme: even the one grand house they had in Radnorshire was destroyed. All that remained, in a field across the valley, were a few sad, wet, ruined walls.

With no sign of the village, I leant Tetley's handlebars and my bottom awkwardly against the bumpy, damp wall of a large house, defended behind its wrought-iron gate by a suspicious sheepdog sitting beneath a Welsh flag, and there wolfed down my cheese and pickle sandwich, plus Boost. A leaflet I subsequently picked up in Cardiff revealed that this house was The Hall, a Victorian Gothic mansion open to pre-booked tours and described as being 'where style meets beauty in a time from the world'. What on earth a 'time from the world' might be I've not been able to discover.

Remounting after just ten uncomfortable minutes, I turned one bend and found myself in the middle of the missing village – complete with comfy bench, picnic tables, information board and pub. An accusing glance at the map showed me that all these features were clearly shown, along with the mischievous bend, and reminded me of the Sixth Law of Cycle Touring:

Your map is your second-best friend (after your bicycle).

Leaning my best friend against the bench, I extracted my flask and, coffee in hand, examined the information board. It mainly concerned the exploits of Owain Glyndŵr, since Glyndŵr's Way, a recently established long-distance footpath, crossed the lane right there.

As the last native Prince of Wales and as the leader of a temporarily successful rebellion against the English, which led to a short-lived independent Welsh parliament,

Owain Glyndŵr has naturally become a focus for Welsh nationalist sentiment. Hence the museum dedicated to him in Machynlleth, first site of the rebel parliament; hence the call for a national 'Owain Glyndŵr Day'; hence the long-distance footpath bearing his name. It criss-crosses the areas where Owain and his men won several battles and it popped out right there in Abbey-cwm-hir next to an ancient petrol pump, nestling amongst the daffodils.

A bold, black-faced lamb clambered up a pile of rubble to baa me on my way. The route became suddenly steeper and, for the first time today, I was obliged to get off and push my way up several inclines closely hemmed in by the dark stands of evergreens that form Coed Sarnau Forest. *Sarnau* means 'causeway' and the next village was Bwlch-y-sarnau, 'pass of the causeway', where the idyllic vale of Clywedog Brook finally gives way to the short valley of the westward-flowing River Marteg.

After a brief break on Bwlch-y-sarnau's already-rotting 'Millennium' seat, I launched Tetley on a long, luxuriously straight downhill, on which the only 'psychling' required successfully removed a rabbit from my path and from which we very quickly reached Pant-y-dwr, where I pulled to a stop before a full-sized palm tree. It stood in the otherwise bare front garden of a modern detached house and was formed entirely of plastic: dark-green plastic trunk, medium-green plastic palm leaves and bright-green plastic coconuts. Breathtakingly tasteless.

In the centre of the village I rejoined civilisation in the form of the B4518 from Rhayader to Llanidloes, but, just as in the previous two villages, it was a civilisation where no one seemed to venture onto the streets during the hours of daylight.

It was severely undulating territory between the valleys of the Wye at Rhayader and the Severn at Llanidloes, but the traffic was light and the frequent pushes pleasant enough between the fields and quiet woodlands. All was quiet until the hamlet of Tylwch, where a blood-curdling scream, as of a child being separated from its limbs, scorched through the tranquillity and had me running over a bridge to a house by the road. There were more frantic screams and a boy of about eight appeared in the garden beside the house, followed by another of about five – the source of the noise – flapping his arms, still attached to his body. They were fighting over a stick, currently in possession of the elder, who announced in Enid Blyton English: 'It's not the end of the world if you never see it again.' With this, he tossed the prize stick into the woods, prompting more cries of agony from his brother and the ominous emergence from the house of their mother.

I plodded on. In running the bike across the bridge, I'd crossed the fast-flowing River Dulas, this one a tributary of the Severn, and entered old Montgomeryshire, named after Roger de Montgomery, one of the Marcher lords. Well before the county was swallowed up by Powys, its county town Montgomery, which challenges Radnor for the title of tiniest old county town, had already been taken over in size by several larger towns in the county, including my destination that afternoon, Llanidloes.

Just before the road finally flopped down into the valley though, the bird population suddenly increased, their squawking eventually being drowned by the noise of machinery and the reason for both becoming evident by the pungent smell of a refuse tip. And there, gliding apart from the gulls and right over my head was a languorous red kite, with its giant wingspan, its distinctively curved, triangular tail and its red-brown body. Ignoring the juicy natural titbits of the countryside near its home, this one had come on a day trip up to the man-made delights of a landfill site.

Descent into the Severn Valley was another brakes-full-on affair and led straight into the back streets of Llanidloes. Before looking for Julie, I remembered my query on the number of the main road and took a quick left to check it out. It was indeed the A470, on its way from Cardiff to Llandudno: *Encyclopaedia* 1, Ordnance Survey 0.

Turning towards town, I was surprised by a familiar face turning towards me. Julie was doing rather an old-fashioned thing: queuing to use a phone box, as Llanidloes is notoriously bad for mobile signals. No longer needing to call me, she led the way to the car park where Tetley was loaded into the Golden Toyota. We had good news to share: hers that our hotel was extremely comfortable and mine that I was too; that this short twenty-five-mile day hadn't brought on the aches and pains of the previous two, which I therefore put down not just to the wind and the gradients but to lack of cycling over the winter. At last, I felt up to the challenge.

Llanidloes is the first town on the River Severn's 220-mile journey from Plynlimon to the Bristol Channel. This location accounts for much of the town's historical wealth – and some of its problems.

The river powered the woollen mills during the boom in that industry in the late eighteenth and early nineteenth centuries. By the 1830s Llanidloes had a population of over 4,000, compared with only about 2,500 today. But the canals that helped the trade further downstream and elsewhere in Wales never reached Llanidloes and local unemployment soon began to grow, prompting the town's most exciting and notorious events in 1839. The widespread unemployment had triggered strikes, supported by the national Chartist movement and, to deal with this uprising, a small number of police were sent from London. They duly rounded up the troublemakers and temporarily imprisoned them in the Trewythen Arms. An angry mob formed and was able to release the leaders by force, effectively imprisoning the policemen in the same inn and controlling the town for five days. Reinforcements were called for, official order was eventually restored and the suspected ringleaders tried, found guilty and transported to New South Wales. Could have been worse – it could have been Old South Wales.

It was at the very same Trewythen Arms, (now known as the Trewythen Hotel) on Llanidloes's main street, that we were staying, but instead of the traditional old inn I was expecting, with the customary swirly carpets and flowery wallpaper, we found ourselves in a palace of cool, soft, contemporary shades. Where I'd hoped for a bar displaying old reports and paintings of the Llanidloes riots was an anonymous beige lounge, from where emerged a rather earnest young landlord to check that we were comfortable, safely parked and knew where to eat and drink. Julie, who knows about these things, assured me that their recent renovation of the inn was faithful to the latest chic ideas, down to every knob, switch and handle, but I must confess to a little disappointment that any local colour had been swept away.

Anyway, Llani – as it is affectionately known by the locals – was itself still full of character and awaiting us after I'd used the shiny bathroom to shower bits and pieces of Radnorshire off the old body.

The evening had turned golden and warm. First call was right opposite the hotel, in both location and taste: the National Milk Bar. I didn't discover this chain of Welsh cafes from the 1950s and 1960s until the 1970s, and Llani's was a fine example: wood-panelled walls, chessboard floors, vinyl-topped tables, all pretentiousness scrubbed out of them. On the wall was the standard, giant map of the NMB outlets, as well as a framed photograph of their founder, R. W. Griffiths, being 'received' by the Queen in 1953. ('Banana milkshake, ma'am?') National Milk Bars have a website dedicated to them by a fan, www.theresposh.com, the joke being of course that, while the NMBs may once have been thought 'posh', they certainly aren't nowadays – and so much the better for it too.

It's odd, but sadly predictable, that tourist guides and websites highlight a nearby stone where John Wesley preached but fail to mention the splendid NMB – or even, in some cases, the riots. Churches and chapels are two a penny (and so you won't find much mention of them in this book), but milk bars, pubs and rebellions... well, they're what life's all about, aren't they?

Having replenished ourselves on, respectively, a lemon meringue and an apple pie, Julie and I advanced further up Great Oak Street, past the grand town hall-cum-indoor market and the timber-framed seventeenth-century Old Market Hall. On Long Bridge Street, we eschewed the delights of the Crown & Anchor, despite the blue plaque intriguingly claiming it to be 'built early eighteenth century, a good example of a seventeenth -century timber framed building' (you'd have to explain that one to me), as well as another inn whose old wooden plaque gave it permission to sell 'intoxicating liquor' only on 'Fair Days, Market Days, Grading Days and Wool Sale Days'. This was because, on the advice of our keen-as-mustard landlord, we were headed for the Mount Inn, another timber-framed job at the opposite end of town.

Entering the inn was one of those 'alien alert' moments, where we were the aliens that stopped dead the only conversation in the bar. It wasn't until I'd ordered and we'd both sat down that the locals resumed, presumably satisfied that we may not be about to exterminate them with a blast from our ray guns after all. Locals they undoubtedly were but, surprisingly, all accents were English and, even more surprisingly, the main topic of conversation was the abysmal state of Heathrow Airport. Rich retirees, perhaps? I wasn't about to find out as there was evidently no way for outsiders to break into this clique, and so we supped up and left.

Our landlord's other recommendation was spot on. Bistro Hafren on Great Oak Street was almost full, served excellent home-made fare and offered reasonably priced wine. Julie took the opportunity to educate me further on the fashions of late twentieth-century Britain. 'Bistros', it appears were the 'in' thing in the 1970s, offering better wine than pubs and decent food at lower prices than most restaurants. Quite why they'd survived (or perhaps re-appeared) thirty years later in Mid-Wales she couldn't say, but apparently their check tablecloths were pretty authentic.

We left the 1970s and crossed the road back to this century's bland decor but, happily, its thick duvets too. Though now confident that my cycling rhythm had returned, I was beginning to feel frustrated at my lack of contact with the locals – a situation that would surely improve the next day, for which I had a prearranged meeting up my sleeve.

Day 5

Glyn and Alwena : Llanidloes to Bwlch y Groes

The town hall clock woke me at seven bells to a grey, damp dawn. Serving our breakfast, our Welsh landlady was oddly taken aback by the rain:

'My, how the weather changes here!'

Togged up for the conditions, I set off downhill and across the Severn, where the riverside properties are safer from flooding now that the river's flow is partially controlled from the Clywedog Dam. North of the river I was immediately out of the saddle and pushing Tetley up the B4569, beneath overhanging trees whose drips mostly drowned the sound of the busy main road across the valley. After less than a mile, the road emerged on the tops again, where drips and traffic rumble were replaced by the multi-tonal baa-ing of sheep and lambs. At one point it was almost operatic as bass and tenor white-faced animals on my left were answered by baritone and soprano black-faced animals on my right. Better than opera, in fact.

Another long-distance path had joined the road in the woodland and, at the top of the hill, it shot off eastwards towards Newtown: the Severn Way, 210 miles of footpath trying to keep in sight of the River Severn all the way from its source to the sea.

Beyond the hamlet of Cerist, an unusually long, fast stretch snaked along a gentle vale as far as the village of Trefeglwys ('church town'). From its name, I'd expected Trefeglwys to be a traditionally quaint place, but a large, footballer-style house called 'Grandstand' and then a number of small new developments suggested that some bureaucrat in a Llandrindod Wells office had circled the place in felt tip and written across the map 'expansion'.

My objective this rainy Mid-Wales morning was to reach a farm near the hamlet of Llawr-y-glyn, some three miles from here up the valley of the River Trannon. Knowing the farm's name but not its whereabouts, I called at the Trefeglwys post office for advice. Never heard of it.

So it was off again, onto a minor road and deeper into the hills. The little traffic that there was soon disappeared altogether, giving the sheep and their offspring full rein to deafen me from all sides until I pulled up by the phone box in the middle of a relatively silent Llawr-y-glyn to review my position.

As with many of my potential wild goose chases, this one originated with an old friend of mine, the Wanderer. The Wanderer is a one-off. If asked his nationality, he'll first consider whether you're a customs officer, a tax official or a friend before replying 'Irish', 'Canadian', 'French', 'English' or 'European', as the circumstances dictate. Likewise, a request for his occupation may bring forth 'writer', 'lecturer', 'geographer', 'meteorologist', 'musician' or even 'skiver' as the whim takes him. All are true. He rarely stays in one place for more than a few weeks but, owning neither diary nor watch, is often unable to predict his own whereabouts for the following week – or even the following day. The previous day has also been known to cause a scratching of the head. My dad met him once and after five minutes concluded, accurately: 'That man doesn't know whether he's comin' or goin'.'

In all things and in all places, the Wanderer wants people to be happy. Sometimes he assumes personal responsibility for this and if he can see an opportunity to bring two or three people together for the greater pleasure of all, then bring them together he will – regardless of any obstacles thrown in his way, including the people themselves. That is not to say that I didn't want to meet Glyn and Alwena – quite the opposite: I eagerly anticipated an encounter with some of the locals, especially given my failure to do so thus far.

At about the same time as I was being motored across the Welsh border at Hay-on-Wye in the late 1950s, the Wanderer (then a child too) was being delivered from the industrial Midlands to this very settlement of Llawr-y-glyn. Like me, he recalls the exotic atmosphere of a remote territory where foreign people with foreign names spoke a foreign tongue. The people with whom he spent many summer weeks here were, I understood, Glyn and Alwena. He'd given me a message for them, named their farm and circled its location on my map.

The wet Welsh rain had stopped and, as I pulled off my waterproof trousers and sat down by the phone box, I noticed that the Wanderer's circle enclosed about ten square miles of Welsh hillside. As I'd already phoned the number he'd given me, with no reply, my next request for help was at a terraced cottage with three bikes propped up outside. A young Englishman answered the door.

'Ah, you've got the wrong bloke, mate. I ain't been 'ere long miself. Try next door.'

Next door, at a slightly more ramshackle cottage, my knock was answered by an English woman with a rather more refined accent.

'Ah, should know, been here twenty-five years now. Erm, now where are my specs?'

She returned from a lounge containing a sofa, a dog and about a thousand knick-knacks, wearing a pair of one-armed spectacles and perused my information.

'Now, er, golly… No, sorry – better try the old man at the mill. He's been here all his life.'

With 'the old man at the mill' I struck gold. He was actually Welsh.

'Ah, *duw*, yes, bit of a climb mind. Right there.' He prodded the map. 'Can't miss it.'

The prod was some way out of Llawr-y-glyn, further up the valley, and so I girded my calves to more pushing. As I pushed I acknowledged some relief that 'the old man at the mill' actually knew Glyn and Alwena, since, to be honest, I'd wondered if they were still alive. After all, the Wanderer was now over sixty, which would put them somewhere in their eighties, at least. I wondered if they'd make it to the door all right?

So it was with some apprehension that I pushed open the gate and approached a modern house at the front of the farm. A decorator was painting the porch and told me that Glyn and Alwena were down at the barn with the sheep. Good, they could still get about then. Having leaned Tetley against the wall, I squelched down a steep, muddy slope and into a muddier farmyard, where an even muddier sheepdog gave me its suspicion-laden, steely-grey stare, while twenty or so sheep bleated their alert from the barn.

'Halloo-o!'

No answer.

'Hallo, anyone there?'

A short, neat, rather pretty middle-aged woman in Wellingtons emerged from the barn and smiled at me.

'Hello, I'm looking for Glyn or Alwena.'

'I'm Alwena.'

'Oh.' My surprise must have sounded like disappointment. 'I mean hello. Er, I'm a friend of Jim Branson's.'

As her smile broadened, a twinkle came to her eye. 'Jimmy *bach*?'

'Yes,' I said, waving a brown envelope, 'and I've got a message from him.'

'*Duw*. A message from Jimmy *bach*! Glyn, come out 'ere! There's a friend of young Jimmy *bach's* 'ere.' The 'Jimmy *bach*' (literally, 'Little Jimmy') was clearly an in-joke, as the Wanderer, six-foot-plus now, must have been a gangly youth back then.

A chuggety-squelch heralded the appearance round the corner of a mud-splattered, once-red tractor, atop which sat a rotund man of about my age, with bare arms and a broad grin. A few more *'Duws'* and 'Jimmy *bachs*' later and we were all back up the muddy slope, boots off and sitting in the handsome kitchen, where a young boy played on his hand-held games console.

'Is this your son?'

Alwena blushed a little at my misjudgement of her age. 'What? No, no, I'm the same age as Jimmy *bach*. This is the vicar's son.'

'Does the vicar live far away?'

'No, he's right behind you. He's painting the porch.'

Tough times in the Welsh church, evidently.

Glyn and Alwena could not have been more welcoming to a scruffy stranger in dirty cycling gear. After coffee was served, cake made available (at the far side of the room from Glyn's eyes, I noticed) and a quick snack from the microwave politely declined, I first asked for an explanation of their evident youth – compared to what, not unreasonably, I'd expected.

The story went that, somewhere in the 1950s, the Wanderer and his cousin came from the Midlands to visit the cousin's cousin, the postwoman of Llawr-y-glyn. With limited scope for entertainment in the village, the two boys often accompanied her on the round, which ended high up on the hillside at this very sheep farm, run by Alwena's parents (not, as I'd assumed, by Alwena herself). The postwoman often stayed for tea and so the boys stayed for tea too. The story thereafter got a little vague, but I infer that Alwena struck up a friendship with the boys, a friendship that had lasted half a century, for they both occasionally still visited or at least kept in touch – in this case, by means of a message from France, written in Spain and delivered from England by bicycle.

Opening it, Alwena read to herself, giggled a bit and said to her husband: 'Well, Glyn, we're not going to sing, are we?'

Glyn concurred. The Wanderer had, I believe, invited them to entertain me by singing plygain, a traditional form of Mid-Welsh carol-singing, with lyrics based on local ballads. Had the Wanderer known a decorating vicar would be on hand?

'No, no,' said Alwena, 'tell me more about Jimmy *bach's* latest adventures.'

I brought them up to date with the man's whereabouts and his tentative dips into actual work, fielded as diplomatically as I could their questions about his latest romances and finally managed to veer them towards their own lives up here on a little lane off a medium lane off a bigger lane off a B-road in rural Wales.

Glyn had come here from his home village about fifteen miles away to marry Alwena, had farmed sheep for many years and was now looking forward to his retirement.

'You know, when a lot of the farmers around 'ere retire, they know nothin' but farmin' and they still talk nothin' but farmin'. Well, I'm not goin' to be like that. What I need's a hobby, isn't it?'

'Any ideas?' I asked.

'Oh, yes. I think I'll try my hand at sheepdog trials.'

'Ah, yes, I noticed you'd got a sheepdog,' I remarked, immediately regretting such a dumb statement of the obvious.

'*A* sheepdog?!' laughed Glyn. 'I've got nine of 'em, man!'

'Are sheepdog trials a big thing around here, then?' I asked, trying to recover some ground.

'Not just round 'ere, man! They're big all over Wales, all over Britain. Sheepdog trials are very popular in America, you know.'

I didn't know that, but did know well enough not to try my joke that all sheepdog trials are a waste of time, because you can tell from their eyes that they're guilty as charged. Instead, the conversation turned to me. When Glyn learned I was originally from Derbyshire, his eyes lit up.

'Oh, we like Derbyshire, don't we, love? Great cakes,' he explained, patting his healthy stomach. 'Bakewell's a lovely place.'

Alwena had seen him eyeing the cakes on the table near me.

'A hobby with some exercise is what you need, Em,' she said. 'Where are you goin' with that bike, Richard?'

I explained my plan.

'*Duw*, it'll take you ages. Don't you need to be back at work?'

'Actually, I'm lucky enough to be retired early.'

'Oh, that's like Jimmy *bach*,' commented Glyn. 'Where do folks get their money from for all these holidays nowadays?'

I explained how I'd managed it at least, exaggerating a little the years of hard work in the overpaid world of computers and underplaying a trifle the hefty dollops of luck in the property market. In short, I'd made the best of being in the right place at the right time.

'Oh, fair play to you, boy, fair play!' admitted Glyn, now rather on the back foot himself.

With the score at about thirty-all, I felt it was a good time to make a move and so, having met Alwena's request for the email address of her old friend, thanked them both for their hospitality and assured them that I'd call in whenever passing again, I said my goodbyes and pushed Tetley back through the gate. The vicar, who evidently didn't deserve a coffee break, was still slaving away on the porch.

Plodding yet further up the hill, and feeling a little privileged to have met such lovely people, I told myself off for having foolishly assumed that things like computers, emails, Derbyshire cake shops and American sheepdog trials would somehow be beyond the ken of Mid-Wales farmers. In the back of my little urbanised mind, I'd imagined that they never left the farm.

This little corner of the Cambrian Mountains was not far beyond Glyn and Alwena's farm and traversed by the north–south B4518, onto which I emerged to turn north once more. The dark rain clouds had cleared, leaving a high layer of lighter-grey stratus still obscuring the sun, and a general air of dampness across rolling pasture dotted with neat white farmhouses, solid grey chapels and puddle-strewn lanes.

Opposite the point where I'd emerged, the meadows dipped down to a corner of Llyn Clywedog, a wiggly reservoir created in the valley of the River Clywedog, a tributary of the Severn. Holding back the waters is a dam that forms Britain's tallest single concrete mass. The reservoir is owned by Severn Trent Water and, as well as controlling the flow of the Severn through Wales and England, it provides water for many in the English Midlands, thus upsetting some of the Welsh, whose valley has been drowned. I thought about the ugly power stations in the Midlands that provide electricity to most of Britain, including Wales, and reflected that perhaps the Welsh hadn't done so badly out of the deal after all.

A keen west wind had got up and did its best to blow me into the path of the traffic as I swooped down a long hill into the village of Staylittle, trying to do exactly that. The route had now taken me over another watershed and into the valley of the River Twymyn which wanders north through the hamlets of Pennant, Bont Dolgadfan and then Llan, where I found a leeward shelter under the church porch for my late lunch. None of these names were familiar to me and, supping some vacuum-flask soup (surprisingly still hot from Llanidloes), I examined both my map and the landscape around. The gentle hills, half covered by bright green fields, half by clumps of darker green trees, were broken by narrow valleys, along which were strung the small settlements, with their solid, stone-built houses and the occasional tiny shop or pub.

This latest watershed was a significant one in the context of the journey, as the stream by the roadside, an almost ubiquitous feature of any tour of Wales, was for the first time flowing ultimately not eastwards to the Bristol Channel but westwards to Cardigan Bay – in this case via the River

Dovey. The map also revealed that the hills opposite where I sat were successfully hiding the giant Carno Wind Farm, fifty-six turbines erected in 1996 and now swishing around to generate enough electricity for 25,000 homes, or fifteen per cent of Powys's consumption. The astonishing scale of each blade had recently been brought home to me when waiting in traffic at Newtown, while a long truck carrying one mounted both pavements to negotiate a quite gradual bend.

Having also taken the opportunity to wring the morning's rain from my socks, pull on a dry pair and resolve to buy some waterproof cycling shoes, I left the little church of Llan (the 'sacred place', dedicated to no one in particular) and pushed on – or rather freewheeled on, as it was still a gentle down-gradient to Llanbrynmair. Knowing this route well, Glyn had promised me, with a glance at the hill behind his farm: 'Just go up there and it's all downhill from the top.'

At Llanbrynmair another scenario by now familiar on this south–north traverse of Mid-Wales was repeated: the sudden, noisy encounter with a main east–west road, followed by a crossing of the railway on the same route, in this case the Newtown–Machynlleth corridor. Scuttling away north again, though, I was soon on another quiet lane, this time unclassified but once again heading into the hills. This topography didn't seem to match Glyn's reassuring comment... until I realised that he hadn't actually said which 'top' it was all downhill from. It's all downhill from any top, I suppose. Beaten by a deft backhand truism, I'd actually left the farm while thirty–forty down.

Pedalling through Pandy, I caught sight of a circular blue plaque on an unassuming terraced cottage. It was the birthplace of Iorwerth Peate, a poet largely unknown outside Wales as he wrote in Welsh, but renowned here as the founder of the Welsh Folk Museum, now part of the National History Museum in Cardiff. A lady smiled at me from the window and, smiling back while pointing at the plaque to assure her I wasn't trying to spy, I pushed off with a wave.

The lane steepened and narrowed as it wound through yet more sheep country, this time with many new-looking wooden bridges across the stream to the left, bridges just wide enough for a man, a dog or a sheep. Wales is home to about eleven million sheep, more than three for each human, and from what I'd seen so far I was surprised the ratio wasn't higher. A later perusal of a Welsh sheep map (yes, you can find everything on the Web) revealed that my route from Monmouth to Anglesey almost exactly matched the line of densest sheep distribution. It's the poor soil and wet climate that make this ideal sheep-rearing country.

As if to confirm it, the weather had closed in again and the rain, so beloved of the sheep but so bemoaned of the cyclist, rolled across the western hills and straight through the slits of my helmet. Reminding myself that generous dollops of rain form an essential part of the Welsh 'cocktail' I was sampling, I whistled my way onward.

Dismounting to squelch along the verge past a pair of parked Land Rovers, I was pleased to hear a sound I'd been awaiting for more than five days and over a hundred miles' cycling: the tuneful lilt of the Welsh language. Although I knew Davies Sanitary, Glyn and Alwena all spoke it, they hadn't spoken it to me of course and this gossiping of the two farmers in their Land Rovers was as beautiful as it was belated.

The stream at this point flowed so close to the lane, and without any barrier between, that just a little more rain would surely see stream and lane as one. Finally bridging the stream, the lane took a last, excessive surge upwards before leaving Powys behind and entering Gwynedd, in the form of the A458 from Welshpool.

Ancient Gwynedd was perhaps the most successful of the ancient Welsh kingdoms – if success is measured by taking over your neighbours' territory. Gwynedd's heyday came in Phase 4 (fifth to eleventh centuries in the Simple History), under the rule of Rhodri Mawr, when Gwynedd ruled almost all of North Wales and much of the south too. Although Big Rod was a bruiser when required – seeing off attacks by Vikings among others – he also took control of some lands by those perennial tricks of the powerful: having the right parents, the right wife and the right deals. Big Rod has been referred to by some simply as 'King of Wales'.

I turned left, joining the traffic headed for the coast, but then right at the Brigands Inn, named after the Red Bandits of Mawddwy, a band of robbers who murdered the Sheriff of Merioneth in 1555. This was not only Gwynedd, but the old county of Merionethshire – and also suddenly and unmistakably North Wales. The landscape had taken a turn for the grander, with giant stands of conifers stretching up towards several 600-metre peaks across the valley of the River Dovey, which I'd just joined. This was a much wider valley than those I'd been pedalling through all day, with the houses on the far side mere dots. Even though the rain had now stopped, the spray from the traffic was heavier and it was with some relief that, just before Dinas Mawddwy, I pulled into our hotel, The Buckley Pines, where Julie was waiting in the car park.

After a short discussion of the weather forecast, followed by an even shorter glance at the sky, I was rapidly back in the saddle again, having dumped most of my kit in the car. My improved physical shape had meant abandoning the Painscastle Pact (a preference for flatter routes where possible) and now one large, unavoidable physical object called Snowdonia lay between my current location (Dinas Mawddwy) and my desired location (Anglesey). At least one serious climb was inevitable and my choice lay just ahead: Bwlch y Groes ('pass of the cross'), the gateway to Bala and the north. The forecast for the next day was, well, awful, but that evening it looked like the rain might hold off – just about. Better a tough, dry end to the day than a tough, damp start to the morrow.

It was eight miles to the top, the last two of which were the climb. Feeling like Hillary making a break for the summit of Everest, I sped through Dinas Mawddwy village, shot past a few isolated, thick-walled houses, bounced up and down over the small undulations on this west bank of the Dovey and pulled up at the phone box in Llanymawddwy, panting and sweating even before I'd started the climb. With hardly any luggage on the bike, I'd gone a little bit mad and was in danger of burning out before the actual challenge. As I resumed, at a rather more sedate pace, the terrain steepened. Waterfalls were gushing off the hillsides to my left and hurtling under the road, even though the map showed each of them draining just a tiny area of moorland. Over to the right, dark-green meadows and then darker-green woods gave way to dark-brown heathland and then mostly bare grey rock below the glowering sky. Way up on the heaths, tiny white specks of sheep wandered about like maggots on a dead carcass. These were no longer the Welsh hills on a springtime afternoon; this was mountain country on a wild night.

About a mile and a half beyond the phone box, the landscape opened out as two high-altitude tributaries of the Dovey joined together and, grunting up the lane that followed the eastern valley, I passed a small sign that said simply, and appropriately, 'Pant'. Banned by my knee-doctor from pedalling out of the saddle, I was soon pushing Tetley up what looked like a 1 in 5.

For less-than-superhuman cyclists like me, who walk our way up hills, there are really only five grades of gradient:

Gradient G1. You're pedalling.
Gradient G2. You're pushing.
Gradient G3. Your only view is of the road.
Gradient G4. The toe of your back foot touches the heel of your front foot.
Gradient G5. Your heels don't touch the ground at all.

Rather surprisingly, this was only a G3 then, although it morphed into a G4 just before the summit. Well, almost the summit. What emerged first from the gathering gloom was an incongruous road junction, complete with signpost. Incongruous because, with no other vehicle at all passing in the forty-five minutes of the climb, I'd drifted into a kind of damp, dank trance where only I, the road and the mountains existed. The suggestion that someone else may come this way snapped me out of it. Beside the junction was a cross, after which the 'pass of the cross' must have been named, and beside the cross a slate plaque telling me that drovers and pilgrims used to pass over here.

Briefly reacquainting myself with the saddle, I crunched along a small plateau into a deserted car park, where an information board marked the summit, though the view it described was hidden by the swirling mists of a North Wales dusk. The car park was awash with puddles and surprisingly ablow with a sudden, biting wind which carried an equally sudden burst of icy rain. Sheltering behind the noticeboard, I celebrated with a single, squishy caramel the achievement at having got myself, my knees and my bike to the highest point of the tour – at 545 metres, Bwlch y Groes is the highest road pass in Wales – before turning back for a rapid, and rather hairy, descent back to the Buckley Pines Hotel, visions of a steaming hot bath dancing before me.

In tune with the surrounding countryside, our hotel was a rather grand, old-fashioned place, with steeply pitched roofs, white walls, and original bay windows and entrance porch. Julie had seen me coming and scuttled out to help stable Tetley in the Golden Toyota. Making sure I'd removed my muddy waterproofs and squelchy shoes in the porch before venturing inside, I could already see that this was just the type of traditional country hotel I'd been hoping to find somewhere along our route: all high ceilings, wide staircases, thick dark carpets and old photographs. Excellent.

Before dinner, things got even better as we discovered the magnificent guests' lounge, with its well-stocked bookcases, deep leather armchairs and views down to the River Dovey and up again to the dark hills beyond, now swathed in mist as well as the gathering night. In the bar, we learned a little more of the hotel both from the wall displays and from the owners, an Anglo-Scottish couple who'd taken over a year and a half before.

Originally the Buckley Arms Hotel, it was built by local landowner and MP Sir Edmund Buckley in 1873 and claims to be the oldest reinforced concrete building in Europe. The original plans on display showed that remarkably little had changed – and thank goodness for that! The Scottish landlord had a few interesting words to say about the star-rating scheme currently run by Visit Wales (formerly the Welsh Tourist Board) and, as this information also appears on the hotel's website, I'm breaking no confidence in revealing them to you here. To achieve a certain star rating, it seems, all the facilities assessed have to meet at least that rating, and all of the Buckley Pines facilities reached at least three stars except, apparently, the lack of a full-time receptionist – even though someone is always in the building and on call. Well, the resultant two-star rating was refused as an insult, but – and here's the bit that was news to me – no one has exclusive rights to the 'star' system and so, whether or not Visit Wales (or the AA or Egon Ronay) assesses an establishment as three-star, this is not the end of the matter: anyone can assess it. So the Buckley Pines Hotel duly assessed itself as three-star, proudly telling everyone why. And good luck to them!

While setting about our three-star dinner, Julie and I reviewed the situation. For the week before our arrival in Wales, and for much of the journey so far, we'd become obsessive consumers of the Met Office forecasts and had to admit that, by and large, they'd been jolly accurate. Our preferred means of access had been the Met Office website (www.metoffice.gov.uk), where you can click your way through the next five days by region and watch the grey clouds, hail and snow merrily put paid to your plans, hour by hour.

'What was the forecast for today?' I asked.

'Vaguely grey with showers,' said Julie.

'Well, that's what we had. Remind me of tomorrow's.'

'Super-grey with super-wet Welsh rain.'

'All day?'

'All day.'

'Hmm. Day off?'

'Yes please! You'd better check if we can stay another night, though.'

A quick word at the bar.

'Day off it is.'

We both drank to that. And, if it could have drunk, so would my drippy cycling kit.

Day 6

A Day Off

Pleased to be ensconced in the metal box of the Toyota, safe from the lashing rain, Julie and I studied the map to choose a route that would offer a tour of the local area. Separated by the massif of Cadair Idris were the dark-green valleys of the Dovey and the Mawddach following parallel, south-westerly courses into the light blue of Cardigan Bay. Such simple map-reading pleasures are denied those who nowadays slavishly obey their sat-nav's commands. Ask your little computer friend not 'How do we get to…?' but 'Where shall we go today?' and it will doubtless reply with an anguished beep. Instead, I asked my little human friend, who was relieved to be navigating passenger instead of driver for a change.

'Well,' she said, 'Urban rather than rural on a day like this, I think.'

'Agreed.'

'And the nearest towns are Dolgellau and Machynlleth.'

'OK.'

'But there's a lump of brown in the way.'

'Cadair Idris.'

'And the nearest way over it is a double-chevron pass called... er... Bwlch Oerddrws.'

'"Windy pass", I think. Just the day for it! Which way?'

'Right.'

Having been rocked and rolled over 'windy pass', the Golden Toyota eventually cruised alongside the damp banks of the Mawddach's tributary, the River Wnion, as we surveyed the small market town of Dolgellau.

'A two-coin town today, I think,' said Julie.

'What?'

'Well, in all the towns I've called at while you've been pedalling through the day, there's been hardly any on-street parking and all the car parks seem to be pay-and-display. So the poor, ignorant visitor has to decide in advance how much to invest in parking before even seeing the town.'

'And what are the two coins?'

'Two quid for two hours. That's the regular rate.'

For the record, the following had been Julie's judgements so far – bearing in mind that it's the pay-and-display system that forces such snap decisions, which may turn out to be quite wrong once you're in the town:

- One-coin towns: Brecon, Rhayader
- Two-coin town: Llanidloes
- Three-coin town: Aberystwyth

Apparently, Builth Wells fell so far below her basic requirements for even a one-coin town that she tried to get away without paying at all.

Our walking route into the centre of Dolgellau took us past Y Bont Fawr ('the big bridge'), whose magnificent, seven-arch span accounts for much of the development of this settlement at the crossing point of the River Wnion, where roads from many directions converge. Another boost was its key role in the seventeenth-century woollen industry, but rather more surprising to me was the news that Dolgellau was at the centre of a Welsh gold rush.

Gold was first discovered nearby in 1862 and the lucky landowner to have a gold mine sunk on his own property was one Watkin Williams-Wynn. Naturally, Sir Watkin was paid a tidy royalty for the gold extracted there, but interestingly he was already so wealthy that he had no need of extra cash and chose to receive his royalty in the form of gold ingots – just for the pleasure of owning such a novelty. Now, there's rich.

As we walked through the narrow streets, however, it wasn't the glister of gold that dominated, but the sober glower of granite. Granite shops, granite restaurants, granite hotels and granite offices. In fact, though home to less than 3,000 people, Dolgellau boasts over 200 listed buildings. While I wandered around admiring them – and engaging in that side-step dance practised by pedestrians with umbrellas – Julie dived into any shop displaying textiles in the window.

In my very limited experience of women, Julie is gifted with a particularly acute version of one typically feminine talent. She occasionally disappears into the spare bedroom, on whose bed has been lying for several weeks a pile of miscellaneous fabric, to emerge a couple of hours later with, for example, a new sofa cover, a new jacket or a complete set of curtains. Some kind of alchemy has gone on in there and, so long as she occasionally emerges with something useful, I don't intend to investigate further. The steady acquisition of the material for the pile, as well as numerous accessories that eventually adorn the end-products – buttons, zips, curtain weights – occurs through visits to towns such as Dolgellau. And here's the strange thing: Julie claims that, at the moment of purchase, she has no idea what the end-product will be.

For myself, shopping holds less interest than just nosing around and I was able to dry out a little at a BBC Wales exhibition, where I learned both that a Bollywood film star had recently moved to the town with the intention of making some films here and that, under blue skies, Dolgellau can indeed look positively sub-tropical. Resolving to return on a better day, I crossed the square to our agreed rendezvous, a quirky looking shop-turned-cafe just off the main square. As soon as I walked in I knew I could happily have stayed here all day.

I believe it had once been an ironmonger's. On the right, a knot of assistants scurried industriously behind a long, cake-filled counter and below a maze of drawers and cupboards.

On the left, a large work surface had been converted into an activity space for young people, who – unusually these days – occupied themselves quietly, co-operatively and without the aid of electronic gadgets. In the middle of the room stood what must once have been the supervisor's office, a glass-fronted cabinet that now housed a selection of books from which customers were evidently welcome to pick and browse. Having ordered a coffee, I picked, sat and browsed. Even the chairs welcomed you in and only reluctantly gave you up.

The pleasure of idle browsing soon gave way to the greater pleasure of overhearing a Welsh conversation at the next table – though only occasionally did I grasp a word or two. We were still in Gwynedd, which boasts Wales's highest proportion of Welsh speakers: sixty-one per cent fluent and seventy-six per cent with some knowledge, according to the 2001 census. Although my own Welsh is almost non-existent, I have at least overcome the two features of the language that seem to put off so many English people. You stop worrying about words apparently full of consonants the moment you accept W as a vowel. And the barrier to pronunciation imagined in the double Ls comes down the moment you relax and simply breathe through the sides of your tongue.

Welsh is a classic case of a language rescued from probable demise by government action: investment, subsidy and legal status. The number of Welsh speakers in Wales increased between the 1991 and 2001 censuses from 508,000 (18.7 per cent) to 582,000 (20.8 per cent), and is doubtless still increasing – with the help of millions of pounds a year to promote it. The argument is usually couched in ecological terms: without help, minority languages would 'die'. In the meantime, Welsh sounds like the lullaby of angels and the place names Dolgellau and Machynlleth like the warm sea breeze that carries it.

By the time the weather blew Julie in too, with the news that she'd upgraded Dolgellau to a three-coin town, I was glazing over.

Our next stop, Machynlleth, lay sixteen miles to the south, along what must, on a clearer day, be a spectacular route over the flanks of Cadair Idris – 'chair of Idris', a mythological giant. Climbing this 893-metre ridge became a popular activity as early as the eighteenth century and was a key factor in the rise of Dolgellau as a fashionable tourist destination. Today, however, blinding cloud lay all around us until just before we crossed the Dovey. Here a watery sun finally pushed its way through to twinkle its weak yellow reflection in the grey, swollen waters of the river, tumbling either side of the 200-year-old bridge – still the lowest road crossing of the Dovey, though nearly twenty miles from the sea.

The town that grew up near this river crossing is Machynlleth – or 'Mach' – now a busy town of 2,000 residents and historically most renowned for having been the place where, in 1404, before representatives of Scotland, France and Spain, Owain Glyndŵr was crowned Prince of Wales. We'd both been here before and Julie confidently judged it a solid two-coin town. This gave me about an hour from parking to our rendezvous and I set off in search of the site where Glyndŵr's parliament was held.

Better known in England until recently as Owen Glendower (after Shakespeare's anglicisation in *Henry IV*), Owain Glyndŵr was born in North Wales in the 1350s, the son of Gruffydd Fychan II – and so, by Welsh naming convention, should have been Owain ap Gruffydd, or Owen Griffiths. Doesn't have the same heroic flavour, does it? He was one of the Anglo-Welsh gentry, studied law in London, served in the English army and took up the position of local squire back in Wales.

In 1400, however, after a typically medieval series of events – disputed rights to the throne, murdered king, treason, that sort of caper – Owain ended up significantly out of favour and severely miffed, whereupon he declared himself Prince of Wales. Actually, his son and his brother-in-law did the declaring but, whatever, the rebellious cards were on the table. Owain's men attacked various royalist strongholds in North Wales: Denbigh, Flint, Welshpool. Henry Bolingbroke (aka IV) had been bowling north to put the Scots to the sword, but news of the princely upstart's actions turned him west via Shrewsbury to slay the pesky Welsh instead. Big Harry had, however, underestimated Owain and Rounds One to Nine went to the Welsh Whacker. Harry regrouped, took Rounds Ten to Fifteen and, implementing a rule unknown even to the teams in Mornington Crescent, cashed in his double score for double digits to claim ultimate victory. Owain escaped, disappeared and was last seen in 1412. A year later King Harry died and his son, King Harry Again, offered Owain a pardon, but even this didn't tempt him into the open. Dead, methinks.

Finding the site of the Machynlleth parliament was not difficult, as it's occupied by Old Parliament House, a sixteenth-century townhouse, nowadays a museum and tourist information office. High on a cliff face behind the building was daubed a slogan that read *'Cymru Ryd'*, which was probably supposed to be *Cymru Rhydd* – 'Free Wales'. On the front of Old Parliament House were two plaques: one to Glyndŵr and one recording a recent visit here by the Queen – I wonder what Glyndŵr would have thought of that.

I headed first for the information office. Closed. I looked around for a museum sign. Absent. The back door was ajar and so I pushed it open to enter a cool, dark, stone-walled hallway. Empty.

'Hellooo! Anyone there?'

Trying not to sound too much like a Saxon invader, I crept up the wide stairs that rose from the hall to a first-floor landing. Deserted. The doors to several rooms off the landing were also open and so I tried my luck again. No one. Not a sausage in the whole building. I didn't try the toilets – maybe the remains of Glyndŵr and his parliament were still in there.

Having scuttled back into the strengthening sunshine, I wandered up the main street. Mach's compact centre focuses on a T-junction occupied by the distinctive arched clock tower, where a plaque records that it was built in 1874 with funds subscribed by the townspeople for – now get this – the twenty-first birthday of Charles Vane-Tempest-Stewart, son of the Marquess of Londonderry, who lived at a nearby mansion. Now, nobody can tell me with a straight face that the local people – from Machynlleth, of all places – did such a bizarre thing without either some behind-the-scenes persuasion or some expectation of reward. No such detail is, however, recorded on the plaque.

After a quick tour of the second-hand bookshops, which nowadays means mostly charity shops, I settled for an early outside seat at our rendezvous, the Maengwyn Cafe, from where I could watch the world go by. An elderly man with a walking stick greeted another of a similar age with a similar stick, saying:

'Mornin', Wynn. I see you've gone lame too.'

A pretty girl of about three danced out of the cafe in a party frock, followed by her mother and grandmother, both of whom proceeded to blow cigarette smoke in the girl's face as they drank their coke and tea respectively. A youth approached near enough for a shouted conversation with the mother in English that revolved around the validity of evidence in an upcoming court case and the wisdom or otherwise of 'taking the rap'. This public discussion then took in another youth across the street – that is to say, he stayed across the street while contributing comments shouted over the top of the traffic:

Meanwhile, the grandmother spoke in soft Welsh to the child.

The arrival of Julie coincided with the re-arrival of the rain and, along with the three generations at the next table, we nipped sharply inside. Over excellent sausages and mash, we reviewed the situation.

'Looks like it's set in for the day,' judged Julie.

'Never mind,' I said. 'I didn't realise I needed a break from pedalling. I think it gets a bit addictive after a few days. My legs have stopped twitching now and tomorrow morning I should be good for another five or six days.'

Day 7

Frontier Country: Bwlch y Groes to Betws-y-Coed

Following another luxurious night at the Buckley Pines and another ascent of Bwlch y Groes (this time with both Tetley and me snug inside the Golden Toyota), Julie and I said our daily goodbyes in the summit car park around eight o'clock. As she returned to a well-deserved plate of bacon and eggs, I hovered for a few minutes to take in the view to the north, obscured two days before by the weather.

A wavy carpet of green hills rolled down to the gentle vale in which lay Bala and its lake, twinkling in some early-morning sun, though the pass itself was still overcast and distinctly cold. In his renowned 1862 book, *Wild Wales*, George Borrow referred to the hills around here as 'the wildest part of Wales'. As an assessment of the harsh, southern side of Bwlch y Groes, I'd have to agree: it was destined to be not only the highest but also the wildest part of my journey. (Not the wettest, though.) Borrow's own tour, on foot of course, seemed to have hit bad weather too, for he described the skies above Bwlch y Groes as having 'assumed a very dismal, not to say awful appearance'. Although he didn't have the luxuries of a hotel into which to retreat, at least Borrow's schedule was more flexible than mine, in that the conventions of the day allowed him to burst into any cottage that took his fancy, dragging the inhabitants from their duties and interrogating them on any topic he wished.

This chilly morning the residents of Cwm Cynllwyd, the northward valley down which I finally set off, seemed to be still wisely and snugly indoors. No movement of the pedals was required for a good twenty minutes as I swished and swayed down the single-track road, braking for a sheep here or a tight bend there. The waterfalls had calmed down overnight to reasonable dimensions and the hills lost their threatening tones. As I pulled over to warm my fingers by a gate, a nervous sheep behind it jumped up and hurtled, baa-ing hysterically into the field, where three or four others joined her to hurtle across to the far side, rounding up several more hurtling colleagues en route and creating a small stampede that squeezed, panic-stricken, through a small gap into the next field, where as many again got the red-alert message and charged wildly to the far side of that field, until about eighty of them were shoving and bleating up against a wall. All I'd done was take off a glove.

The temperature must have notched up a couple of degrees every five minutes and by the time I emerged in the sun to see my first car of the morning at Llanuwchllyn, it might have been pushing double figures.

Buenas días, Llanuwchllyn, *buenas días el sol…* for this was the birthplace in 1822 of Michael Jones, a prime mover behind the establishment of Wales's famous Argentine outpost, Porth Madryn. The key factor wasn't anything particularly unique about Argentina but rather its distance from the influence of England. Jones and his colleagues had investigated many locations around the world in which to establish a Welsh colony, including Palestine, before eventually reaching an agreement with the Argentine government for a hundred square miles of Patagonia. Many of the 153 settlers who left Liverpool in 1865 came from the Bala district, pushed by agricultural evictions and poverty. Though Porth Madryn has since become Puerto Madryn, Welsh is still spoken there today.

Llanuwchllyn's other claim to fame lay a few hundred yards beyond the road, its name-board glittering back up at the blue sky: the southern terminus of the Bala Lake Railway. Wales has more preserved narrow-gauge railways than you can shake a signal at, but this four-and-a-half-mile line beside the lake up to Bala is actually a remnant of the standard-gauge Great Western link from Wrexham to Dolgellau. A little blue diesel shunter marshalled four red carriages into the platform as I turned right to take the B-road parallel to both railway and lake.

Nowadays called Llyn Tegid, Bala Lake is Wales's largest natural lake, occupying the middle part of a glaciated fault-line valley drained by the River Mawddach beyond a low watershed to the west and by the River Dee, through the lake, to the east. The irregular stands of trees that fringed almost all the lakeside were still mostly bare, giving glimpses of the choppy surface as I rolled along the road to the south. In some stretches, wind-blown reeds and grasses reached out into the lake, their yellows and greens playing against the deep blues and blacks of the lake; in others, the hillsides plunged straight beneath the surface at an angle that gave no worries, it appeared, to the sheep munching idly a few yards above lake level. Yet it seemed that this corner of the natural world had had a bad night, as first a dead rabbit, then a dead lamb and finally a dead female mallard lay stricken at the sides of the road. Beside the duck, her male partner stood a mournful guard and perhaps had stood there all night. No boats of any kind were to be seen on the lake until just before the eastern end, where one or two dinghies heralded the Bala Sailing Club, where I took advantage of a small pebble beach for a swig of drinking water and a finger-dangle into the lake. Icy cold, both. If a future 'Time Team' were to dive this edge of the lake, they may find the remains of ancient sandwich wrappers and school uniforms. A friend of mine who attended Dr Williams' School for Girls at Dolgellau in the 1960s tells me that, en route home by the old lakeside railway at the end of each term, the girls would despatch their carefully prepared spam sandwiches into Lake Bala– to be followed, en route home when finally leaving the school, by their school hats.

With a population of about 2,000, Bala is big enough to have what may loosely be called suburbs and it's through one such that I cycled in, past another cyclist carrying home his Sunday newspaper, past a gaggle of churchgoers and past the silent, curtained windows of a backpackers' hostel. After my early start, it was some real, non-instant coffee I was after and I was therefore pleased to spot a hotel on the main street with a few stragglers still at breakfast. Having placed my order, I sat in the lounge's ample sofa, inspecting the map and anticipating the coffee. The arrival of a cafetière was a good sign, although the waitress's urgent insistence that I press the plunger 'extremely carefully' was not. After two minutes I carefully plunged and the coffee carefully spilled all over the shiny table. When the waitress, evidently miffed at my ineptitude, had brusquely wiped up about half the mess, I poured the coffee and observed about a thousand little grains swimming around in my cup. They'd evidently used filter coffee instead of cafetière coffee. Having sipped a little (it was awful), I paid up for the sake of the warm, comfy chair and was off.

With two of the town's main features being a Calvinist theological college and a statue to the founder of the British and Foreign Bible Society, and with this Sunday morning lending the town an eerily abandoned atmosphere, I felt no encouragement to hang around and soon pedalled out of town. I'm sure Bala's quite a different place on a busy summer afternoon.

The A4212 formed a steep hill between the college and a school, before settling down parallel to the busy River Tryweryn. It was a pleasant valley scene, with smooth sheep pasture rolling past tall, bare trees down to the meandering stream, where... where it seemed that a giant magpie was beating its giant wings as it flew down... no, wait a minute... As I pulled up, the magpie morphed into a series of kayakers circling their multi-coloured paddles high in the air as they manoeuvred their way around rocks and rapids. Informative as ever, my map told me that a mile or two upstream lay the National Whitewater Centre and, since then, their website has told me that, because the flow of the Tryweryn is controlled from a dam holding back Llyn Celyn, this river often has enough water for rafting and kayaking when others in Britain do not. During this ride, lack of water had seemed a problem very unlikely to appear on the Welsh horizon.

Turning right at Frongoch, I followed the smaller valley of the Tryweryn's tributary, the little River Mynach, into the lonely, wild hills once more. Giant boulders were strewn over the fields, glacial erratics dragged here by the ice thousands of years ago. The further I cycled, the fewer were the signs of even the twentieth century: a yellow grit bunker, a stack of hay bales neatly wrapped in green and white plastic and a tall, red silo declaring 'Honey Nut Only'. But that was about it. All the little farm buildings looked centuries old, the fields themselves centuries older.

Just after the turn-off into an even narrower lane, a tidy farm called Hafod-yr-Esgod had placed a traditional, naked haystack right where I wanted it, close by the road, by a babbling brook and next to a sawn-off, seat-sized log. The hayrick was presumably one just released from last year's stock and offered a convenient shelf for my vacuum flask and sandwich bag. So there I sat in the noonday sun of an early spring day, supping hot carrot and coriander cup-a-soup, munching marmalade sandwiches and staring out over some of the gentler Cambrian Mountains. The golden hay and soft sky seemed to herald summer and I let my mind wander to the possibility of sandy beaches and outside tables later in the trip...

Right now, I had to go to Ty Mawr Cwm, 'big house valley', the only place marked on the map in the five miles between here and the next main road, and so, after the pleasantest wayside feast so far, I packed up my things, ensured nothing was left to show my passing, and pushed on further uphill.

Despite the better temperatures, strips of snow still lay in sheltered hilltop curves to the west. The unclassified road threatened to turn into nothing but a track as a grassy strip developed in the middle and then a gate barred the way. For the first time on this trip I wondered if I might have taken a wrong turn, but, with the map confirming no other route, I opened the gate and passed through. Almost immediately another first made me look pretty silly, as a sudden down-slope on the gravelly surface proved such a challenge to the brakes that, to avoid careering straight into a farmyard, I rammed my left foot into the grassy bank to bring Tetley and me to an unglamorous stop, half in, half out and half over the hedge. Yes, three halves. It was just my luck that this was in full view of the only other human I'd seen in about an hour, the farmer at what must have been Ty Mawr Cwm, crossing the lane on a small caterpillar tractor. I waved, he grinned. I freewheeled off, he caterpillared off.

Up and over another ridge and I'd finished my four-day frolic through the Cambrian Mountains. I had emerged in a tributary valley of the Conwy, a north-flowing river emptying into the Irish Sea less than twenty miles away. A fresh wind had blown up and the mountains of the north had also made a sudden appearance, snow-topped and cloud-tipped across the western horizon: Snowdonia.

As I pushed up to the main road I was surprised to see no road sign, but happened to know that the choice was either right for Marble Arch or left for Holyhead and Dublin, since this was the A5, one of the six principal routes radiating from London. As my father explained in those pre-motorway days, when first showing me how to read a map, the road numbers of England and Wales take their first digit from the segment where they start, the segment being defined by the principal route where it begins, in a clockwise direction. Thus most of Wales's road numbers start with a four, as most of Wales lies between the A4 and the A5. Those in the northern segment I'd just entered, however, start with a five. To prove it right there at Pentrefoelas, the road off the A5 to the south was the B4407, while the one to the north was the A543.

Pleased that some logic still remained in the world, I set off not towards Marble Arch but towards Holyhead, slowly getting used to the unusual presence about me of other road users. The A5 itself has a proud history. It was designated as a continuation of Watling Street, the Roman road from Dover to Wroxeter (now in Shropshire). Despite the road improvements of the eighteenth century, in 1800 it still took at least three days to travel from London to Holyhead, a route used regularly by Irish MPs, as Ireland was politically part of the UK by then. The worst section was this North Wales stretch and in 1815 Thomas Telford was commissioned by the government to rebuild the road, complete with toll booths – and with a bridge across the Menai Strait to Anglesey. After fifteen years, Telford had delivered, establishing himself as one of the great engineers of the age. Using the same route he developed nearly 200 years ago, the one-time three-day trek now takes about five hours. I guess the horseless carriage may also have contributed to this improvement.

This particular corner of North Wales seemed a jumble of frontiers, spatial and temporal, as I'd not only slipped into the historic county of Denbighshire (Phase 7 of the Simple History – sixteenth century), but also into the slightly more recent (but now defunct) county of Clwyd (Phase 9 – twentieth century) and the current county of Conwy. Over the last few decades, the local councils must have used up their entire budget in letterheads alone.

Hoping I'd exhausted the list of boundaries just crossed, I pulled into a pub at Rhydlydan, only to be proved wrong. It was a strange-looking place, like an enlarged council house with an unsympathetic, flat-roofed extension and a large pond between the pub and the hammering traffic of the A5. The man who suggested where I put my bike, the barman and the middle-aged customer in the frilly mini-skirt (a lady, I should add) all had the same accent: 'Over dare, mate', 'Worrel you 'ave?', 'Dat's grrrreat.' Scousers.

Lacking its own sizeable city, all of Mid- and North Wales tends to orientate either towards Birmingham and the Black Country or towards Liverpool and Merseyside, whose citizens in their turn tend to orientate for relaxation towards the nearest part of Wales. Down in Dolgellau and Machynlleth, most of the English accents were Black Country. Somewhere else along today's ride, I'd also crossed the linguistic boundary into the Liverpool hinterland.

After a short discussion with the barman about whether I was allowed to have a mere snack on a Sunday lunchtime (a 'Maybe' followed by a reluctant 'Yes') and after paying an exorbitant amount for a dry jacket potato, I quickly ate up and left. A back road to Pentrefoelas looked the quieter option but a sign announced that the bridge on the road ahead was closed. A muddy Land Rover was coming from that direction and I stopped to ask the driver's advice.

'Can I get across the bridge on a bike?'

'I just come across in this, so you'll be all right, boyo', said the farmer.

'Why do you think there's a sign then?'

'Oh, it's always the same. They seem to put 'em up round 'ere just to give the council boys something to do.'

As I crossed the bridge, completely open and free of road works, I noticed 'the council boys' supping coffee in a van while their weekend's time-and-a-half mounted up.

The six-mile run up to Betws-y-Coed was pretty easy going, though thronged with vehicles, a few of which now bore Irish registrations en route to or from Holyhead. The River Conwy itself thundered in from the left, then the Machno and the Lledr, so that by the time I crossed the waters on Telford's Waterloo Bridge, the river was a mature, wide and rock-strewn feature. As its bold, white inscription states, the bridge's elegant arch was indeed constructed in 1815, although the whole bridge was not complete and in use until some time afterwards. Only the seventh cast-iron bridge in the world at that time, it formed one of the most triumphant parts of Telford's road improvements. Even today, the view from the bridge up and down the deep, tree-lined valley is a most inspiring one.

Betws-y-Coed ('prayer house in the wood') was the most touristy place I'd pedalled through and the continuing good weather had brought a fair few of the milling visitors out onto the terraces of the cafes and bars strung along the main street – in fact what looked like the only street.

My initial destination was the local bike shop to pick up some more brake blocks. The cheery, tattooed assistant offered me a straight replacement pair for £4.99 or 'a better deal' in the form of a more expensive pair where you could replace the actual rubber blocks instead of the whole part.

'And how much will the rubber blocks be?'

'Er, £6.99. Ah, yes, what we'd call not such a better deal after all, sir.'

No. To extract himself from his financial hole, he offered me a number to call for bike advice from anywhere in Wales. Card carefully pocketed.

We'd booked into Glenwood, a guest house on the far side of town, and there was Julie, sunning herself on the lawn of an attractive 1930s house, complete with curved bay windows unusually framed in wood rather than metal. The couple that ran the place broke the record for our landlords on this trip so far: they'd been there all of four years, having bought it from a long-time lady owner and carefully retained as many period features as possible. Inside it smelled as my aunt's house in Slough used to in the 1950s – not an unpleasant smell and one which Julie put down to the furniture polish.

Hitting town for the evening, we identified two old coaching inns as possibilities and, adopting what had become a standard plan, checked out the first while downing aperitifs, but keeping the second up our sleeves if the first didn't shape up. This time we definitely needed the back-up, as the first had managed to ignore the grand view from its front bay windows by locating its bar at the back in a tiny, squashed annex with no view, no customers and, as soon as he'd served us, no barman. The second was a much better bet and here we settled to our fish and chips and red wine to review the day and plan the next.

'Did you come up over Bwlch y Groes again after breakfast?' I asked.

'To be honest, I didn't fancy those steep, slithering roads and thundering waterfalls on my own, so I toured out to the west and then back again to Bala along the north bank of the lake.'

'What did you think of Bala?'

'Mmm. Strange, bleak, closed... a one-coin town. Better on a summer's day with an ice cream and sun-hat. One to come back to, I think.'

I was glad it wasn't just me.

'The forecast's pretty good for tomorrow,' she went on, having been listening eagerly on the car radio.

'If we had to choose just one fine day in all the rest of the tour, I'd choose tomorrow.'

'Why?'

'Well, Snowdonia's notorious for being cold, windy and largely invisible – but on a good day, I reckon it's one of the best places to be in Britain.'

'I didn't know you'd been here much.'

'Well, just once to the top of Snowdon, to be honest. Spectacular climb up, disastrous walk down.'

'What happened?'

'Hidden rock, broken leg – not mine, one of the sixth-formers I was leading – helicopter rescue, the whole caboodle... it'd be nice to associate Snowdon with something good again.'

Day 8

Slices of Paradise: Betws-y-Coed to Menai Bridge

The Met Office had done it again: not only sunny but calmer, the morning looked promising. Julie had chosen the Llanberis Pass and I the Nant Ffrancon, further east and shorter, the two routes diverging at Capel Curig.

Historical documents claim that Telford lowered the steepest gradient of the A5 through Snowdonia down to 1 in 22. Well, if the road out of Betws-y-Coed to Capel Curig is 1 in 22, then I'm the Queen of Sheba and command those historians to put their toe-clips where their quill is and try pedalling up it. It was a pleasant enough walk though, especially as the view of the Swallow Falls on the River Llugwy is free to cyclists and pedestrians: just walk past the turnstile and look over the wall. Not just the view but also the sound as, for a change, the bleating of sheep had been replaced this morning by the relaxing babble of water echoed in the trees at almost every turn.

More items of interest came pretty rapidly. Just past the falls, the so-called 'Ugly House' turned out to be nothing of the sort, but rather a nice little stone cottage close to the road. The story goes that this substantial building was thrown up overnight in the fifteenth century, thus qualifying under a law of the time as a *tŷ un nos* ('one-night house'), for which the builders – two brothers in this case – could claim the freehold for free. I imagine it picked up its 'ugly' description from the multi-sized and multi-shaped stones of its outer walls, and in order to pull in the punters of course – but if you want ugly buildings, then more will come in a few days.

On this old turnpike Capel Curig was the next place for coaching inns after Betws-y-Coed and, I would guess, the last chance to rest or change the horses before the long haul to the top of the pass, about six miles beyond. I pulled up at one of the inns myself, not to change horses but for some coffee and advice. My map's legend was in Welsh and a cycle track I hoped to use further on was marked as *'Llwbr beicio wedi'i arwynebu'*. *'Beicio'* was obviously the Welsh for bike, and I knew *'llwbr'* was path, but the rest?

Alas, I'd chosen the wrong inn, as the chap in charge, though keen to help, was another Liverpudlian.

Leaving Capel Curig, I could see Snowdon itself along the Llanberis route, unusually clear, suitably snowy, almost Alpine. George Borrow went so far as to characterise Snowdonia as the 'British Alps' and, indeed, just a few miles south of Snowdon at Nant Gwynant lies the headquarters of the International School of Mountaineering. On my own route to Nant Ffrancon, the woodland was suddenly gone and wide expanses of mountainside lumbered in front of me, the top hundred metres or so also spattered with snow and the lower slopes occasionally broken by an isolated house or a ruined barn. On my right two heavily laden young hikers were getting last-minute map instructions from an older man before they headed up to Llyn Cowlyd, one of Wales's most isolated reservoirs. On my left, half a dozen distant, multi-coloured moving dots were already well into a ramble among the huge boulders that lay scattered below the intimidating slopes of Glyder Fach and Glyder Fawr, towering up to just an arm's length short of a thousand metres.

Telford's gradients were pretty good here and I was able to pedal most of the way up to Llyn Ogwen, where two youths walked by separately, each staring at the pavement, each plugged into an iPod whose tinny percussion I could hear and which they clearly found more diverting than the landscape. At the far end of the lake, which is also the top of the pass, there was a surprise waiting for me.

My faithful map had told me there was a youth hostel here, but had failed to mention the minibuses, the hundred or so healthy young persons, the geology exhibition, the food kiosk and the slices of paradise. It was an outdoor pursuits centre.

Being solidly Welsh, the chap in the kiosk was able to tell me that *'wedi'i arwynebu'* means 'surfaced' and also that, should I care to fold the map over, I'd find an English translation. Duly humbled, I took my Paradise Slice (prepared by The Wicked Cake Company) and my steaming coffee into the geology shelter and there found a lanky youth with wild hair and earrings staring closely at the information panels that explained in some detail the glacial history of Cwm Idwal, an area to the south-west of here. When his mouth wasn't hanging loose, it was saying to himself:

'Amazing. Wow.'

I read alongside him and asked 'Are you here on a geology trip?'

He raised his eyebrows (also wild) and admitted, in a London accent, 'I came for the laughs, but now I think I'll look out for the geology.'

'There's a lot of it to see round here.'

'Yeah,' said Lanky, still staring in astonishment at the panels. 'Someone's actually worked all this out.'

Good luck to him. Maybe Lanky will work even more out for future generations.

Cwm Idwal's certainly a classic location for seeing with your own eyes the dramatic legacy left by the glaciers of the last Ice Age, which finished only about 12,000 years ago. The power of glaciation comes not only from the weight of the ice itself but also from the force of gravity dragging it downhill and the erosion caused by the material dragged along with it, which acts on the landscape around rather like the hard gemstones in a giant drill head. The *cwm* itself (and this Welsh word is used beyond the confines of Wales) is the scooped-out basin at the head of a glacier, now occupied by the metallic blue lake of Llyn Idwal. The startlingly steep tributary valleys that flow into the lake are called 'hanging valleys' because the lower valley is so much lower that the tributaries appear to 'hang' high up in the surrounding slopes. Other glacial features in this area include huge scree slopes, containing the waste material from violent erosion, and hummocky 'moraines', left where a glacier has slowed down and simply dumped vast amounts of the surface material it had been carrying. It's all textbook stuff, but so much more impressive in the flesh than in the classroom.

Ignoring the main road that takes the east side of Nant Ffrancon for its descent to Bangor, I pushed Tetley behind the youth hostel and freewheeled down a track that hugs the west flank: NCN 85. I was soon stationary again, as three long-tailed, Welsh mountain ponies approached to smell my shoes and Tetley's tyres before giving us the OK to carry on. Another hundred metres and I was off the bike again, to answer the questions of a muddy, southbound cyclist about the cafe facilities ahead.

'Does this route go all the way to Bethesda?' I asked, still not sure about the dotted cycle-route symbol.

'It does indeed,' said the cyclist in a plummy, Home Counties tone. 'And the quarry section is quite good fun, too. By the way, when you pass another chap on a bike, tell him to get a move on, will you?'

Passing his friend a little farther down the hill and relaying the message, I received the wry reply:

'Huh. The man's just too fit for his own good.'

Finally coasting uninterrupted along the track, I was able to take in the spectacular scenery of the glacial vale of Nant Ffrancon. Great, grey peaks soared on both sides from the flat, green valley floor, where the River Ogwen meandered indecisively and boggily northward. So steep and rugged were the flanks of the hills hereabouts that no feature but rock, moss and the occasional sheep was discernible. The only toe-holds of civilisation were strung along the two slender, parallel routes of the A5 and my own narrow track: a farmhouse here, a gate there. Running alongside the track was a form of fencing I hadn't seen before, made from vertical strips of slate, about twenty centimetres wide, strung together with wire. The state of both slate and wire suggested the fencing was far from new.

As the track swung right to rejoin the main road, a cycle-route sign invited me to ignore it and continue straight ahead through a gateway and along a dirt track. In doing so, I was joining the section marked on the map as 'surfaced', a confusing attribute, since it had been surfaced – without the symbol – all the way to here anyway. As another cyclist approached – a helmetless bald-headed man of about my age – I raised my hand to ask his advice about the route he'd just ridden. Sliding his rather rusty machine to a halt, he considered me for a few seconds, then the question for a few more, before finally putting his thoughts into words.

'Surfaced? Well, yes, there's a surface,' he explained slowly, in a strong Birmingham accent. 'The surface is slite. Pieces of slite. Local slite. From the slite quarry.'

'Oh, this is the quarry, is it?'

Examining me carefully again, Slow Brummie evidently decided that I was one or two spokes short of a full wheel, for thereafter he embellished every comment with further explanations of the key word he'd used, to make sure his messages had got through.

'Oh aye, a big quarry. A big 'ole in the ground. Trucks goin' in and...' – he squinted as though about to reveal a state secret – 'and trucks comin' out. Full, and I mean full, of slite. Welsh slite.'

'That's a sturdy old bike you've got there,' I said, trying to veer the conversation away from the hot topic.

Having cast his eye over his bicycle, the valley, the sky and finally me again, he suddenly declared: 'Gorrit out of a skip.'

'Oh...'

'A big metal container. They tike 'em away on trucks. From outside houses.'

'You did well. Have you had any problems with it?'

Another Pause.

'Mmm. No brikes really. Nothing to stop me. Birrof a challenge comin' through that slite. Walked most of the way. Lorra the time, the boike's just a circular walkin' stick really. Don't wear an 'elmet though. No 'at. No 'ard 'at. 'Elmets are fer pansies.' He glanced at mine. 'Suits you though.'

I laughed.

'I mean...' said Slow Brummie, realising his faux pas, 'I mean loik, er...'

'It's all right', I grinned, not really wanting to know what he meant this time. 'Better pansy than dead, eh?'

We parted and after a few metres, hearing a bang, I looked back to see that Slow Brummie's free, brakeless bike had reached the gate. Having found hardly anyone en route to speak with for seven days, they were now coming thick and fast. When a man walking southbound with a Labrador appeared round the next corner and suddenly asked, in a Scouse accent this time, 'Are the dogs out?', I just slowed down to say I'd seen no dogs for several miles, before pedalling on. No time to learn what dogs he meant: I had a quarry to cross.

Slate is a fine-grained, metamorphic rock and its usefulness comes not only from its durability and imperviousness but also from the ease with which you can split it into convenient, flat shapes. It's a natural for roofing. Penrhyn Quarry falls in the 'Great Slate Belt', which also takes in Dinorwic Quarry in the Llanberis Pass, now closed. Developed by the Pennant family in the late eighteenth century, Penrhyn employed 3,000 men by the 1890s, led to the creation of nearby Bethesda, effectively a company town, and supplied the slate to roof much of northern England's terraced housing. Reputed at one time to be the biggest slate quarry in the world, Penrhyn is still being worked, nowadays under the ownership of an Irish construction group.

Riding through just the edge of Penrhyn Quarry site, it felt more like a slate mountain. It was an extraordinary sight. For about two miles, the left edge of the cycle track was bordered by huge piles of slate, towering grey into the sky, as though just left there by the devil's dumper truck. Some pieces of slate were the size of picnic tables, others just tiny shards – with all sizes in between. The track itself was covered in small pieces of slate and the slope continued to the right, partly slate-covered and partly rough grass, as it tumbled down to the River Ogwen, which at points churned along perilously close to the crumbly edge of the track itself. There were barely any fences and no warnings that I saw. In the USA there would have been armed guards at either end of the track handing out health and safety warnings. As it was, I was delighted to career across such elemental terrain at my own risk... even though it felt as though the slightest rainfall would send the whole mountain, Tetley and me crashing into the river, to be disgorged a few hours later as a battered wreck into the Irish Sea.

Instead, NCN 85 disgorged me safely onto a B-road that led to the village of Tregarth, where the local school displayed a banner declaring 'Tregarth schoolchildren say "Show you care and park elsewhere."' Just beyond, a sign invited me to leave the road and take the Lôn Ogwen, a cycle path that would carry me beside the River Cegin 'as though you are walking hand in hand with the river' before 'passing languidly over the viaduct'. An offer I couldn't refuse.

It was certainly a pleasant enough route. Its first stretch followed a disused railway track, converted into an easy gravel path through gentle meadows, before turning north, still on a comfortable gradient as it wiggled under the busy A55. From here I followed the well-signposted cycle path as it struck through the woods on a dry route a few metres above the River Cegin, but from where a number of slate paths led to the bank of the river itself – in case you wanted to walk hand in hand with it. Finally, the Lôn Ogwen threw me onto an unclassified road which the river crossed on a ford, to the delighted squeals of two children in the back of a Renault Scénic that splashed through it with the windows down. Pedalling carefully across the river and up a steep hillside, I was taken aback to see, beyond the fields and the roofs of suburban Bangor, a misty blue glitter that I'd forgotten I was heading for: after eight days cycling across Wales, here was the sea. Conwy Bay in fact, with the tiny stump of Puffin Island to the left and the breadth of the Irish Sea beyond.

I soon found myself in the back streets of a Bangor council estate, from where a team of road workers directed me to the Menai Bridge. The one I crossed was the older of two: that elegant suspension bridge on which Thomas Telford drove the Holyhead road across the Menai Straits in 1826, one of the earliest suspension bridges in the world. With a tidal range of up to eight metres here, it was no surprise to see a strong current swirling past but it was something of a shock to lean over and see how far below me it was. It was therefore with some care that I walked Tetley off the island of Great Britain and onto Anglesey. It was with some regret as well, since it meant the end of the day's ride through Snowdonia, truly one of Britain's most spectacular regions and much better seen from the saddle of a bike than from the seat of a car. I felt sure I'd soon be back to see it in the best way possible: on foot.

With the opening of the bridge, the small community of Porthaethwy changed its name to Menai Bridge and is now the third largest settlement on Anglesey. It was here that we'd made another unseen booking – and had another success.

After her own Snowdonia crossing, Julie was waiting at the Auckland Arms Hotel, an inexpensive option where we'd both been expecting a rough-and-ready room above the bar. What we got was a spacious, airy and modern room on the ground floor, complete with TV, DVD player, sofa and coffee table. The landlord, a young and efficient Englishman, seemed to be not only manager, receptionist, barman and waiter, but also – according to Julie, who knows about these things too – local heart-throb, for next to our dinner table in the bar, a table of giggly girls kept him in view, testing his patience with one ridiculous drinks order after another. Unflustered, he dealt with them all, with us, with all the locals – and, I should imagine, with a few major problems of the free world in his spare time.

We felt we were in safe hands for two nights.

Day 9

Ynys Mônotonous: Menai Bridge to North Point

After the spectacle of Snowdonia, my route across Anglesey was – how can I put it without upsetting the tourist board again? – scenically challenged. For this, I really had only myself to blame. It's not that I wasn't aware of the island's interesting corners: Edward I's remarkably well-preserved castle at Beaumaris, the constant majestic backdrop of the Snowdon range on any tour of the south-east coast, the broad views and sheltered beach at Red Wharf Bay... In fact, Julie and I did manage an evening spin in the car out to the characterful old Ship Inn, set on its perfect site right on the edge of Red Wharf Bay. No, the problem lay in planning and in knees.

My target was the most northerly point of Wales – near Llanlleiana Head, beyond Amlwch – and back again. With Anglesey having only two neighbouring access points (the Menai crossings), some doubling back seemed inevitable and my examination of both the map and my B&B lists two days before seemed to point inexorably at Menai Bridge as the spot for a two-night stay. So far so good, as the Auckland Arms was outstanding. The downside of this plan, however, was that the intermediate day, at nearly fifty miles, would probably be the longest of the tour. Twenty years before, a fifty-mile day in the saddle would have been a breeze, but my knees had since caught up with me (an intriguing anatomical achievement) and now fifty miles meant a full-day slog, probably no time for scenic diversions and certainly the most direct route possible: out along the B5111 through the middle of the island and back down the A5025 that skirts the east coast.

Looking on the bright side, though, this would all be virgin territory and so, with a cloudy but dry start, I pushed Tetley up the gradient out of Menai Bridge in good spirits. The higher I climbed the windier it got. At some roadworks on the outskirts of town, the foreman's paperwork constantly threatened to escape his clipboard. At the first sheep field, most of the inmates were crouched low down against the leeward side of their drystone wall. As you'd expect on an island jutting out into the Irish Sea, it was a westerly wind that had bent the hedges and trees over the years and which today forced the crows to fly backwards and buffeted a northbound cyclist into the path of the traffic.

You may read elsewhere that Anglesey is the fifth largest island in the British Isles. Not true: they've probably forgotten the two biggest. It actually comes in at number seven, after Great Britain, Ireland, Lewis/Harris, Skye, Shetland's Mainland and Mull. At 276 square miles, however, Anglesey is by far the largest island in Wales. In the 2007 international Island Games, held on Rhodes, Anglesey came fifteenth, well above bottom-placed St Helena, but some way behind table-topping Jersey.

Plenty of standing stones, a 4,000-year-old burial mound at Llanddaniel Fab and other pre-historic remains are testament to the island being well settled during Phase 1, before 600 BC. The Celts of the next phase developed an important druidic teaching centre on the island, which became a major druid stronghold. Putting an end to all this, though, were the Romans, who eventually destroyed the local druids' centre on Anglesey in AD 61 – despite the short-term success (according to Tacitus) of a fiendish druidic tactic wherein they waved their hands in the air and shouted vicious curses at the invaders. I bet that put the wind up the Latin lads.

Other early invaders included the Irish and of course the ever-popular Vikings. In fact, the name 'Anglesey' probably comes from the Old Norse Ongl's ey, the island of Ongle. And who was Ongle? No one seems to know. The Romans called Anglesey 'Mona'; the Welsh themselves call it Ynys Môn. And where does this name come from? No one seems to know that either.

Trundling along the B-road between Llangefni and Llanerchymedd, my own theory was that *môn* was short for *mônotonous*. Sheep field after sheep field, hedge after hedge, wall after wall, farm after farm... The low plateau that forms Anglesey's interior is neither hilly enough to be interesting nor flat enough to offer much in the way of views. At least I felt I was off the beaten track – which after all, I reminded myself, was one of the objectives in choosing a rather oddball route around the principality. As if to confirm this, I noticed that Anglesey County Council hadn't bothered putting up any distance signs along this road, presumably on the assumption that only locals would be using it. So the only clues to my progress were a few landmarks – windmills, mining headgear, a rare, two-storey white house – that swung into and out of view as I battled along in a little windy world of my own. A lone front-gardener encouraged me with 'A cold day for yers!', but no one else was around. Llanerchymedd – literally 'sacred place of the windblown traveller' – was completely deserted. Actually it means 'sacred place of Erch the mead' and there's a rumour on several websites that some of the locals believe Jesus Christ's mother, Mary, was buried here. Funny how the wind – or possibly the mead – affects the brain.

Compared to what had gone before, the town of Amlwch arrived as an oasis of fascination: streets, shops, roadworks, people. This was contrary to the view of someone we'd spoken to in Menai Bridge that morning, who'd asked:

'Where are you off to today?'

'Amlwch.'

'What on earth for?'

'I'm headed to the northernmost point of Wales. What's Amlwch like?'

'Dunno. Never been.'

'How long have you lived on Anglesey?'

'Six years.'

'Why haven't you been to Amlwch? It's one of the few towns on the island.'

He considered this for a while, before concluding:

'Nuthin' there.'

There used to be lots here. Amlwch grew in the eighteenth century with the development of nearby Parys Mountain, where the copper mines were once the most productive in the world. During the 1780s, this area dominated the global copper market, sending its ore to Lancashire or South Wales for smelting. A strategic value of the metal at the time was its vital use in the construction of 'copper-bottomed' warships, including *HMS Victory*. One side effect of Amlwch's copper boom that still remains is its impressive harbour; one that doesn't is a remarkable ratio of four public houses to each inhabitant at the height of the boom.

Actually I was headed to a pub myself, and a rendezvous with Julie at Bull Bay, just outside town. The seaside inn boasted a panoramic view of the Irish Sea and a wonderful, steamy vegetable soup, but suffered from a barmaid with a curiosity bypass.

'Not very busy for you today?' asked the blue-helmeted cyclist, evidently on a long-distance ride of some kind.

'Uh?' responded the barmaid.

'I bet you'd rather there were a few more customers – or are you happy just to look at this magnificent view? It's the first open sea I've seen for days.'

'View? Uh. The bill?'

To confirm that my somewhat negative impression of Anglesey was not a one-off, Julie had had a frustrating morning in the car too. Repeatedly egged on by road signs directing her to the beach, she found herself on a single-track, beachside road with no parking places and thrown straight back onto the main road. Time and again. Driven instead to distraction, Julie planned a trundle around the shops at Menai Bridge instead, accurately comparing a drive on Anglesey to that old sixpenny game where you try and get a little silver ball through the maze and into the hole, but always end up tilting it down some cul-de-sac or other.

No trundle round the shops for me. Instead, the tantalising proximity of Wales's northernmost point urged me back into the saddle and, against a strengthening westerly, out of Bull Bay on the Cemaes road, then north on an unclassified lane until that finally gave up the ghost near a farm called Llanlleiana. Here I had to leave Tetley locked up near a stile while I, my blue bag and my map case continued on foot.

Being without shoulder straps, the big saddle bag was a big nuisance and I clutched it awkwardly as I lumbered in my small cycling shoes across two bumpy fields and, via a steep path, up the gorse-covered hill on whose sides once stood the Celtic hill fort of Dinas Gynfor. Pausing for breath, I turned to see, just a few hundred metres to the west, the later remains of a china clay works at the side of its associated little harbour, Porth Llanlleiana. At the crest of the hill, a number of paths spread out through the undergrowth and I took the one that led north-westwards, directly into the teeth of what by now amounted to a gale. My hat was already in my pocket and now my glasses joined it before they flew into the sea. Head down, I pressed on, now only yards from my target. I was almost upon the old tower before I saw it. Well, some kind of lookout tower is what it appeared to be, but it turns out it's a ruined summerhouse, built in 1901 to celebrate the coronation of King Edward VII. Its greater significance to me was that it sat on the northernmost point of Wales accessible without the use of a boat – not that there was anything there to tell you this. While the headland about 250 metres to the west is called Llanlleiana Head, this northernmost one seemed to have no name at all.

'*Pen Gogledd,*' I muttered to myself. 'I hereby name you *Pen Gogledd*. North Head.'

Sitting myself and my luggage on the leeward, though still very blowy, side of the dilapidated structure, I took in the view. Wind-strewn seagulls danced over a dark blue sea that stretched, choppy and agitated, to a hazy horizon below a lighter blue and now cloudless sky. On a clear day, they say you can see the Isle of Man and the Lake District from here. Not today. Very clear to see though, less than a mile away, was Middle Mouse, a tiny uninhabited islet on which St Patrick was allegedly shipwrecked before swimming ashore on Anglesey. If it's true, fair play to the boy. Today it would have taken a miracle to swim that stretch of water, with Middle Mouse's western tip covered in the spray from crashing waves.

After managing to pop a Minto into my mouth and its flapping wrapper into my pocket, I struggled to my feet, extracted my camera from the other pocket and, holding the camera tighter than I'd ever done, took a few wobbly pictures to prove that I'd made it. While squinting through the viewfinder I was lucky to spot my blue saddlebag begin a wind-driven, eastward roll and scuttled over to rescue it – taking great care where I stepped, for beyond a pile of rocks that must once have been the summerhouse's outer wall, the flattened carpet of heather and bracken fell steeply away to the sea. I briefly wondered how long it might take Liverpool City Council to trace the origin of a battered body washed up against the Pier Head. With this wind speed, I'd probably still be warm on arrival.

Photos done, I would happily have hung around, taking in my success at covering the 200 or so miles from Wales's easternmost to its northernmost point in eight days' cycling – except that hanging around wasn't the sort of activity encouraged by a gale that now made it difficult even to keep my feet on the ground. And so, after painstakingly zipping all loose items into their allotted pockets and taking a quick last glance at the dancing undergrowth of this wild, wild spot, I set off back down the track, this time bracing my back against the best efforts of the wind to hurry me into the next cove: Hell's Mouth.

Everything looked different this way round. Was that the track down the hill? Or was this almost identical one the right route back? Yes, this gorse bush looked familiar... but then so did that one over there. So did they all. At one point, I actually headed off in the direction of the ruined summerhouse again, but, just managing to keep a few grains of logic lodged inside my head, finally picked the shortest – and steepest – route down the hill's inland flank and landed with a stumble and a bump onto the path across the fields. Yes, indeed it *is* funny how the wind affects the brain.

Happily reunited with Tetley and refreshed by a swig of cold water, I shot off – an hour or two behind schedule, but now propelled south-eastward by a gentler wind that had transformed itself once again from enemy to friend. As I bounced back onto the main road, I wondered if I was the only person ever to have headed out here simply to stand at the northern extremity of Wales. The lack of any notices or signs identifying it – just as at that distant, but particular spot by the River Wye – suggested that maybe I was.

Having sped through the outskirts of Amlwch, I embarked on the long stint down Anglesey's east coast, which managed – remarkable though this seems – to be even more featureless than the interior. The Internet subsequently told me that it was seventeen miles down to Menai Bridge, but the secretive Anglesey Road Sign Department did its best to keep this information from road users.

With the shore itself too far away to see, I cast around desperately for something to hold my attention, but my wandering eye was continually drawn back to the giant lettering which appeared on the road surface every hundred metres or so: 'ARAF SLOW'. I tried to deduce which features they felt justified the advice to ARAF SLOW down and I'm pretty confident I can now reveal them to you. You must go ARAF SLOW every time you approach a building. You must go ARAF SLOW every time you pass a lamppost, a hedge or a tree. You must go ARAF SLOW if the road is steep, if the road is level, if it is bendy or if it is straight. In the unlikely event that none of these features appear, you are recommended to go ARAF SLOW just in case they are about to do so.

As it was, all I can report for my seventeen miles is that, so far as can be seen from the main road, the village of Pentraeth has three shops: one selling educational toys, one selling computer support and one selling vinyl floors. Rather frustrating if you actually want bread, milk and a newspaper, I should imagine.

It was almost sunset before I swung with some relief into the Auckland Arms and, fifteen minutes later, swung out again, showered, clothed, arm-in-arm with Julie and intent on a pint or two. First, though, we strolled up and down Menai Bridge's main street, past an interesting collection of independent shops – this in itself being a very welcome contrast to the 'identikit' high streets that have crept into most parts of Britain. Julie's favourite in Menai Bridge was an ironmonger's, where she admired a classic shopkeeper's office, complete with high wooden desk and many-labelled drawers. Further on we were drawn to a stationer's window display which tempted us with his latest stock of sheep registers, goat registers and cattle movement books. This led us neatly to a flight of steps that in turn led to the lounge of the Victoria Hotel, a room decorated with atmospheric photographs of sailing boats where an atmospheric drunkard leaned half-on, half-off the bar, assuring everyone that he would be returning home 'quite safery by pubric trasport'.

Julie had bought a copy of the local *Holyhead Anglesey Mail* (established 1881), which we jointly browsed, eager to discover how Anglesey residents staved off boredom. Unsurprisingly, having a pop at Anglesey County Council was one common pastime, for the latter had just brought in a daily boat-launching fee of £10 for locals to use public slipways, access to which had previously been free. Going to the chip shop offered another potential source of excitement, for John Williams of Cemaes Bay had 'joined the fish-frying elite from across the UK' by winning a national quality award. To qualify, his shop had been thoroughly inspected by a 'seafish-approved inspector'. How the seafish had approved the inspector was not revealed by the *Holyhead Anglesey Mail*.

Over in Holyhead, however, violence had recently been on the agenda, for Jedi Master Jonba Hehol (when not dressed as the master, also known as local hairdresser Barney Jones) had been attacked in his own garden by none other than Darth Vader. Fortunately, the incident was captured on video and local police confirmed that they recognised the attacker immediately – well spotted, the Holyhead police! It's just possible, of course, that the assailant may only have been dressed as the fearsome cyborg. However, a colleague of Hehol's, Jedi Master Yoda, declared later 'Predict this I did... Beware the Sith.'

Enough! Dinner called and this evening it was to be an excellent sausage and mash, washed down by acceptable wines and beers, at the Liverpool Arms. We were entertained by the obsessively detailed account of a weekend with her German boyfriend recounted in twenty-first-century schoolgirl English by a wide-eyed teenager and listened to with infinite patience by her heroic parents – and the rest of the bar.

Our own conversation turned to the meaning of Liff, a game based on the 1983 book *The Meaning of Liff* by Douglas Adams and John Lloyd, wherein real place names are imagined to be ordinary words and suitably sounding definitions invented for them. The subject came up because we'd known the pub was quite busy from the loughborough we'd heard (loughborough (noun) – the burble of meaningless talk that passes through the window of a pub when the bar is full.) And after my long day on the bike and a couple of pints, I'd soon gone to melksham: (noun) – the place where we appear to have gone when staring vacantly into space.) These were our own inventions from previous games.

After two days on Anglesey, Julie had realised the meaning of it. Anglesey (noun) the vaguely anxious state in which you sometimes awake, knowing that everything that day is going to go wrong.

Day 10

Sustrans Does its Job: Menai Bridge to Porthmadog

Although I woke up still in Anglesey, I didn't wake up in *an* anglesey (as defined the previous evening), since that morning I was a Cyclist with a Challenge.

Sustrans has been lacing Britain with a National Cycle Network for many years now but, although a fan, I find I rarely follow one of their signposted routes for more than a couple of miles. The first reason is that many, if not most, of their routes are in fact roads, shared with other vehicles.

The second is that their routes often take me where I don't want to go. The latter had already been happening regularly on this trip, where an east–west NCN route would briefly join my south–north route and then wander off again.

That grey, wet morning, things were about to change. I'd noticed that my intended route down to Porthmadog and beyond more or less coincided with NCN Route 8 and so I'd challenged myself to follow its little blue-and-red signposts all the way, unless presented with a compelling reason not to.

With a wind warning on the Britannia Bridge, I once again walked across the suspension bridge, happy to be escaping Ynys Mônotonous. Looking west you get a good view of the sturdy yet now strangely inelegant Britannia Bridge. Designed by Robert Stephenson and opened twenty-four years after Telford's suspension bridge, the structure had to be re-engineered after a catastrophic fire in 1970, started by burning papers dropped by teenagers who were using them as torches to search for bats. The reopened bridge included a road deck on top of the original railway, which now carries the A55, part of Europe's E22 from Dublin to Sweden.

As I rejoined the mainland, the rain stopped and I was already on NCN 8, which here follows the A487 westbound – and immediately found my resolve tested. While my logical route continued on the straight and level main road, Sustrans's little '8' sign directed me left, up a severe gradient to goodness knows where. Gritting my teeth, I dismounted and pushed uphill. A series of twists and turns followed, eventually leaving me at an unsigned fork where two traffic-free paths headed westwards: one uphill, one downhill.

Knowing that I was ultimately headed for a coastal track, I took the lower path, only to find myself after a few hundred metres facing an impenetrable fence.

Sustrans 1: Guise 0

Shouldering Tetley, I climbed a flight of steps to regain the upper track and from that point had to admit that the route was a good one. After hugging the Menai shore through Port Dinorwic – the old outlet for slate exports from Dinorwic Quarry and now reborn as an area of trendy waterside apartments and renamed Y Felinheli – NCN 8 had found a disused railway trackbed to whisk me all the way to Caernarfon. Various information boards told me that NCN 8 was also Lôn Las Cymru, a 250-mile cycle route right across Wales from Holyhead to Cardiff and Chepstow. Throughout my time on NCN 8, I saw only one sign visible from a road that tempted the passing motorist with a 'Cardiff' sign pointing down a quiet cycle track.

This shore-side route along the old railway gave me an excellent start to the day. For four miles I crunched along the gravel track, on my right the waters of the Menai Strait, now calm after overnight rain, on my left a mixed landscape of rich green pasture, isolated white farmhouses and low wooded hills, beyond which the rising flanks of Snowdonia disappeared into the low cloud. Though the rain had stopped, more looked likely – and I felt I'd better enjoy the conditions while I could. The cycle track brought me into Caernarfon beside a giant new block of flats, from which the views over the Menai Strait must be fabulous, but *of* which the view from Anglesey is, I can assure you, ghastly – since Julie and I had driven down the opposite shore two evenings before. With Edward I's magnificent Caernarfon Castle having dominated this end of the strait for nearly 700 years, twenty-first-century man has managed to blot it out inside a decade with a tasteless lump of concrete that, I predict, will be enthusiastically demolished before the end of the century.

For 2,000 years Caernarfon has been an important administrative centre, from Roman Segontium to county town of Gwynedd, as it is now. In 1954, when Welsh local authorities voted for the first official capital city of Wales, Caernarfon finished second, with eleven votes to Cardiff's 136. Of its 10,000 population in 2001, eighty-six per cent spoke Welsh, the highest proportion of any large community in the country.

I'd already visited the town several times, but on the last occasion, four years before, I was sorry to see how dilapidated it had become – and therefore especially pleased to note its apparent renaissance this time around. Castle Square was being pedestrianised and I sat outside a cafe there, happily supping a cappuccino. There's something about arriving in a town on a cycle track that puts you in a good mood, and the way the rays of the watery sun played on the handsome façades of the square reminded me for some reason of the old cathedral square in Barcelona. Must have been something in the coffee.

As I walked over to examine the statue of David Lloyd George, for fifty-five years Caernarfon's MP and for six years Britain's only Welsh prime minister (so far), two of the workers from the square approached in their fluorescent orange jackets.

'Do you know why that statue's unique?' asked one of the other, in a heavy North Welsh accent.

'No,' said the other.

'Well, Lloyd George himself was 'ere at the unveilin'.'

'So what?' His mate had put into words exactly what I was thinking.

'So what?! You don't know anythin', do you? Statues are supposed to be put up to people who're already dead. Didn't you know that?'

'No.'

'I bet this gentleman 'ere did,' he said, waving at me.

I had to admit I didn't.

'God!' exclaimed our informant. 'Am I the only smart person in this town?'

Cheered yet further by this banter, I freewheeled down to the harbourside for a better look at the castle. With the Welsh being skilful at ambushing overland convoys, many of King Edward's castles were built on the shore to protect coastal supplies, as well as fulfilling a defensive role for the local English settlement and garrison. But in the case of Caernarfon Castle, another role was just as important: this massive structure physically dominates the town and strait and was intended to be a symbol of English dominance over the Welsh. A political statement as much as a military one. As I stood admiring the sturdy longevity of the various towers, an American tourist, stepping down from a coach and turning, awe-struck, to take in the structure, summed it up perfectly in a comment to his wife:

'Now that's what I call a castle!'

Pushing Tetley along, I made a full circuit, walking out above the small beach where the River Seiont flows into the strait and then back along the streets where twenty-first-century small-scale business carries on in the shadow of this testament to thirteenth-century power struggles.

Remounting, I scooted down the slope in front of the Queen's Gate again, now in search of NCN 8's exit from town. It was a grand one. Next to an unsightly new shed that marked the Caernarfon terminus of the Welsh Highland Railway (WHR) stood an ornate wooden archway bearing the image of an old bicycle and the name Lôn Eifion, presumably a local section of Lôn Las Cymru, aka NCN 8. Cycling beneath it I joined an excellent stretch of cycle track – level, newly surfaced, fenced, and well signposted – that ran parallel to the WHR for a few miles as far as Dinas, where rail route and cycle route diverged. Every summer, apparently, this stretch of the path hosts a 'race the train' charity run.

The north-east corner of Wales is a hotspot for narrow-gauge railways and the WHR is its biggest recent success story. The original line having closed as long ago as the 1930s, the project to restore it began in 1961 and, as I cycled beside it forty-seven years later, was very nearly complete. (Latest news can be found at www.welshhighlandrailway.net.) As I passed Dinas station, the diesel locomotive Castell Caernarfon was working a rake of carriages into place while a young woman with a trolleyful of on-board refreshments waited to cross the track, singing lustily into her mobile phone: 'Good morning, good morning, good moooorrrrninnnng... to you!'

South of Dinas, the gradients remained gratifyingly gentle as the path followed the trackbed of an old London and North Western standard-gauge line across the neck of the Lleyn Peninsula. Dense woods on each side squeezed the cycle track into its own long and narrow universe, where every one of the few passing cyclists raised a confidential eye to acknowledge a fellow traveller. Where the trees thinned out, the outside world came back into view. On the right, tiny settlements of grey stone houses speckled the low green hills as they swept away westwards to the distant, blue-grey line of Caernarfon Bay. On the left, lower and lower cloud hid any view beyond the damp slate roofs of the nearest village.

NCN 8 had by now started to 'walk hand in hand' with the main A487, not the quietest of companions, and I soon started looking for somewhere to turn off for a snack. A sign pointing to 'Village Centre', without revealing which village this may be, pointed over a footbridge to the east and I followed it.

The street led between some shabby houses, past a pub called Yr Goat whose 'Croeso' (welcome) sign lay above a pair of firmly-locked doors, into a small square where a recent shower had failed to wash anything clean, and as far as another pub, this time permanently boarded up. The only life I'd passed was a fish and chip shop in the grubby square and so there I returned and entered. The Chinese lady who served me had a nice smile, but apparently little English beyond 'chip and pea mix open', and so, with my sorry level of both Welsh and Chinese, I tried to strike up a conversation in English with the only other customer, a teenage girl with earphones. As she either didn't hear or didn't want to, I returned to the square, selected the only two-foot length of bench without any dollops of unidentifiable mess and set about my chip and pea mix.

Even though I'd experienced only five minutes of this small town, which a glance at my map revealed to be called Penygroes, it immediately shot into fourth place in my lifetime list of the Worst Towns I've Visited in the World, pushing Spain's Empuriabrava (a Disney-like, mock-classical town spoiling a beautiful bay) down to fifth. The top three remained the same: at third-worst, the strip of giant, garish hoardings that is Laramie (Wyoming); at second-worst, the boarded-up, post-industrial landscape of Middlesbrough (England); and still at No. 1, the Very Worst Town I've Visited in the World was Dowlais (South Wales). Poor, grey, featureless old Dowlais had held that position for over thirty years and as I finished off my mix, which was not at all bad actually, I wondered if I'd get the chance later in this trip to reassess it.

Scurrying back past Yr Goat, I regained the relative beauty of NCN 8 and scanned my map for anywhere more interesting on my route south to Porthmadog: one Nebo, two Gravel Pits, three Burnt Mounds and a Bodychain. Hmm. Not exactly enticing. Actually, this was another slate-quarrying area that I was passing through, although nearly all the quarries around here had closed. A little farther on I crossed what was once the border of Dwyfor, the last 'dry' area of Wales. It was not rain but the sale of alcohol that Dwyfor banned on Sundays from 1989, by means of a law passed in 1881 that allowed this to be decided locally. For many years, Welsh counties were known to be either 'wet' (Sunday drinking permitted) or 'dry' (banned). Dwyfor, a last stronghold of the Welsh Sabbatarian temperance movement, sneaked in as a short-term administrative district from 1974 to 1996, when Dwyfor's abolition released its would-be Sunday drinkers from their purgatory – or perhaps sent them there. The law was finally repealed in 2003.

This stretch of NCN 8 was scenic enough without any diverting settlements. It cruised on its gradient-free way through dark woods where the slightest birdsong echoed long through the boughs, then curved gradually west and south again, revealing different aspects of the rolling hills to the west and of the winding Dwyfach Valley to the east, until it suddenly split between the Criccieth branch of NCN 8 and the Porthmadog branch. Taking the latter, I found myself thrust once more into the hills, past disused quarries, quiet farms, looming old woollen mills and unfortunately, at the corner of one field, a dead cow trapped in the mud from the night's rain.

The route into Porthmadog passed through its suburb, Tremadog, birthplace of T. E. Lawrence. A rather unexpected second connection between Wales and Lawrence of Arabia is revealed in the *Encyclopaedia*: several of the desert scenes in the 1962 film of the same name were not shot in Arabia at all, but in the sand dunes of Merthyr Mawr Warren, south of Bridgend.

'Port', as the town of about 4,000 is known locally, was bustling with late shoppers as I pedalled down the main street and into our digs, the Tudor Lodge, which Julie had already assessed as conveniently located, eminently comfortable and outstandingly organised. The shower worked too and we were soon on the lookout for some refreshment.

Porthmadog developed after the Cob, a long seawall, was built in 1811 by William Madocks to reclaim a large portion of the beach for agriculture. It became a busy port, with slate brought in by rail from Blaenau Ffestiniog and from the slate quarrying area I'd passed through earlier. Nowadays it's tourists that dominate, attracted by the marina, the restored railways and Port's location as a gateway to the Lleyn peninsula and Snowdonia.

Rather surprising, then, that the main street was stubbornly unforthcoming on the public-house front, offering only a rowdy-looking local decorated with a porchful of tattooed bruisers. Just along from there, the town's former National Milk Bar had changed hands but still looked a fair bet for coffee and cake and so we gave it a try. Twenty minutes later we emerged from a 1960s time capsule, overcome by a sea of custard-coloured plastic furniture, stunned by a three-foot-high luminous meringue, bemused by the choice between 'licensed restaurant' and 'unlicensed restaurant', but happily filled by four Bakewell tarts and two frothy coffees.

A back-street pub called Y Llong (The Ship) soon calmed down our senses with a pint of Tetley's and a glass of Merlot. In fact, with my lunchtime chips and teatime tarts, I was glad that Julie had already bought some light nosh for a lazy evening in front of the telly at the digs. I think by nine I'd gone, dreaming of Lloyd George eating luminous chips in a Chinese opium den.

Day 11

Not a Number, but a Free Cyclist: Porthmadog to Aberdovey

The Tudor Lodge's breakfast room reached further heights of organisation as cupboards opened here and tables pulled out there, pre-loaded with all the paraphernalia for a healthy, self-service breakfast. I was especially grateful for the lack of cooked breakfast among the options, saving me that particular daily battle with the devil, and enjoyed the healthy fruit salad and yogurt instead.

The weather had taken a turn for the better and for the first time on this trip I set off without either coat or trousers. I still had shorts on, of course. As I cycled across the Cob on its landward side, a light morning breeze carried the sharp smells of gorse and seaweed, along with the trickling sound of an incoming tide passing under the cycle track. Leaving Porthmadog also meant leaving old Caernarfonshire and re-entering old Merionethshire. Impressed by yesterday's Sustrans route, I aimed to stick to it again wherever reasonable. While the main road carried the morning traffic to Penrhyndeudraeth and the rest of the world, good old NCN 8 took me on a short tour of some quiet back lanes before pointing me over the Glaslyn estuary by way of a short toll-bridge, the keeper waving me through as a free cyclist. From the far side of the bridge, I stopped to look up and down the estuary, where the shrinking sandbanks were dotted with birds – too far away to identify – dancing from one bank to another as pools and rivulets changed the shape of the sands, even as I watched. Parallel to the south bank of the estuary, short grasses and gorse formed a thin cover to the cracked and mossy rocks which muscled up to dominate the landscape to the east.

Three miles on, at Ynys, I turned right. Having ridden down to the shore, I walked out onto the tussocky grass, laced with tidal channels that wiggled away to Traeth Bach ('little beach'), beyond which the sea sparkled in front of a shimmering Mediterranean-style village. In the late 1960s, this particular location was a subject of weekly fascination for me, as for many others. Known simply as 'The Village', the settlement featured as an enforced retreat for troublemakers in Patrick McGoohan's TV creation, *The Prisoner*. McGoohan himself played the central character, 'Number Six', and the opening sequence terminated with him standing defiantly on these very sands, raising his fist to the Welsh skies and shouting words I now called out myself, forty years on – after first looking around to check that no one was listening:

'I am not a number, I am a free man!'

To those not caught up in the TV series, the village across the water was – and still is – Clough Williams-Ellis's artful creation, Portmeirion.

Two miles back, Sustrans had tried to point me into the contour-infested interior of Merionethshire, but this time I'd stood my ground to stay with the coast road. I am not the NCN 8, I am a free cyclist! While the officially recommended route laboured through the hills, I cruised along the straight and flat main road to Harlech.

Sustrans 1: Guise 1

As I approached Harlech I craned my neck to take in Edward I's 700-year-old castle – it looked freshly built and as good a template for a sandcastle as you could want. If it had actually been the thirteenth century, though, I'd have been cycling underwater, as the castle originally stood on cliffs that fell away directly to the sea, which nowadays lies about half a mile away, beyond a golf course. In 1404 Owain Glyndŵr held court here (at the castle, not the golf course), having taken the stronghold that same year. The town of Harlech, which used to be the county town of Merionethshire, lies behind the castle and therefore up a series of steep streets, which, with another long day on my hands, I decided not to tackle, continuing instead along the main A496 and gradually climbing, to enjoy some breathtaking views back over the flatlands to the Glaslyn estuary.

While the distant view was majestic, the immediate roadside view was scarred by one of the worst examples of modern architecture you're ever likely to set unfortunate eyes upon. Theatr Harlech looks for all the world like a rogue spacecraft that has crash-landed upside down, attempted to deploy its stabilising legs, failed and then been left to rust, its rocket boosters still pointing skywards and, for all we know, its little green life-forms still rotting inside. What makes this gruesome building even worse is its location amid such beauty, both natural and man-made. If 'Visit Wales' wants another item of interest to tourists, it might pull up the signs to the 'Ugly House' near Betws-y-Coed and transplant them here, offering guided tours of a building that boasts ugliness on a much grander scale – and with better views, so long as you're looking outwards. To be fair to the theatre itself, its range of activities seems remarkable, with productions in both Welsh and English, musical recitals, hip-hop workshops, sing-a-long operas and regular films from around the world. Maybe after a while you don't even notice the building.

With the road still rising, I asked a woman who appeared from the back of Theatr Harlech how far the hill went.

'Oh, a few hundred yards,' she said. 'But after the downhill there's another bugger – and then another. This is Wales.'

Fair comment.

Having tackled just one more of the 'buggers', I turned right in Llanbedr and pedalled quickly down a quiet lane towards the seashore, keen to visit somewhere I'd had on my mental hit list for several years – ever since a friend had described in such glowing terms the idyllic place where he and his family had spent many a happy summer holiday: Shell Island.

Shell Island is actually a raised peninsula at the northern end of Morfa Dyffryn beach and is home to what, at 300 acres, is reputedly the biggest campsite in the UK. It's big enough to practise 'wild camping', with pitches well away from your nearest neighbour and with permission for campfires on the beach. The beach itself is said to be home not only to birds and wild flowers, but to 200 types of shell. All in all, it sounded a great place to be on a fine day – and today was fine enough. My plan was to cycle into the camp, walk through it if necessary, emerge on the beach and then set off down the seven miles of surfaced cycle track marked on my map as part of NCN 8 and running parallel to the beach right down to Barmouth.

That was the theory. The reality was a sudden realisation why it's not called Shell Peninsula. The lane I was following was marked on my OS map as crossing a ford just short of the camp. For 'ford' read 'sea'. Before my eyes the tarmac of the lane disappeared beneath the waves of Cardigan Bay, then the boulders marking the edge of the lane disappeared too. Both re-emerged a good 200 metres beyond, next to the first buildings of the 'island'. What I could see was that the tide was still coming in. What I couldn't see was how deep below the waves the lane had sunk. Another bugger, then.

Though a sign part way along the lane had announced 'Tidal Causeway', the two boxes below it, marked 'CLOSED' and 'OPEN', had been equally empty. At the junction with the main road in Llanbedr, there'd been no sign at all – of either information or warning.

Sustrans 2: Guise 1

With an 'assist' from the Ordnance Survey.

Reluctantly, I retraced my wheel tracks and set off back down the main road. In Tal-y-bont, however, another opportunity presented itself to access the illusive beachside cycle track, in the form of a half-mile link from the main road, which I eagerly took, passing through a caravan site, complete with its fully flashing amusement arcade but minus all its customers. Once again the lane disappeared in front of my eyes, this time into a steep bank of pebbles, which I climbed on foot to find myself on an empty shingle beach. A sign advised me that the shingle 'forms an integral part of the coastal defences and the removal of stones is THEFT.'

I stared over the grey bay, then up the grey beach and then down the grey beach. No NCN 8. No sign of a cycle track – unless a few recently dug holes were the beginnings of it. So if I'd have got across to Shell Island just before the tide swallowed the road, there'd have been no exit route anyway and I'd have been trapped for hours by a combination of Sustrans and the Ordnance Survey. A lucky break, but...

Sustrans 2: Guise 2

En route back I called in at the caravan site's cafe to celebrate my escape from Shell Island with a cup of tea and a currant bun, but its tea lady had evidently been to the same surgeon as the Bull's Bay barmaid for her curiosity bypass.

'Bit quiet here today,' I ventured.

'Anything else?'

'No thanks. Any news of the cycle track along the beach?'

'That'll be £1.90 please.'

Bun between my teeth, I was quickly in the saddle again.

The northern route into Barmouth (or Abermaw: 'mouth of the Mawddach') is not its best feature, but its long grey promenade did present a passing mystery in the form of two recently abandoned theodolites about half a mile apart: The Strange Case of the Murdered Surveyors? Just before town, however, the prom was enlivened by a long line of palm trees in sturdy tubs, each sponsored by a Barmouth business: this one by the HSBC Bank, the next by Williams' Garage and the next by the Mermaid Chip Shop. As I was passing one of the Mermaid's competitors, a familiar golden Toyota swung alongside, with a beaming Julie leaning out of the window. Pure coincidence.

Over plates of sausage and chips, we compared our morning's notes.

'Did you come along the beach path?' asked Julie.

'There is no beach path, it turns out. But the flooded causeway stopped me getting trapped on Shell Island.'

'Oh, it was just clear by the time I got there.'

'What's Shell Island like, then?'

'Who knows? It was a fiver to park on the island.'

'Blimey, they must be mad.'

'My thoughts exactly. I got out fast. But anyway, I'd already spent a beautiful half-hour on the beach at Llandanwg. Free parking too.'

As we chatted, two Barmouth council workers began shovelling wind-blown sand into wheelbarrows and returning it to the beach. The younger, about eighteen and significantly overweight, returned from his first trip (about thirty metres) crimson-faced and panting. This job might be the making of him.

From here to Aberdovey, where we'd booked for the night, our routes would diverge, as she would be forced to follow the River Mawddach inland almost to Dolgellau, while I'd be scooting over the cycle track that hitches a lift over Barmouth railway bridge. And I knew that this cycle route was a real one, not just a figment of Sustrans's imagination.

The further south you go in Barmouth the better it gets, with the small, lively harbourside area the best of all. Here, cheek by jowl with tea rooms and seafood cafes, are the Harbour Master's Office, the Yacht Club and the quayside itself, with its small fleet of fishing boats, its miscellaneous pleasure craft, and the gaping and gossiping that enliven all harbours around the world, big or small. Every June it's packed to overflowing for the start of the Three Peaks Yacht Race. Not to be confused with the Three Peaks Race, this one does require scaling the same peaks (Snowden, Scafell Pike and Ben Nevis), but involves calling at them while *sailing* from Barmouth to Fort William. The little business of getting from deck to peak is achieved on foot and bicycle.

Barmouth's website (www.barmouth.org.uk) claimed that their town is 'seeped' in a rich history. Walking up the road to the bridge, I kept an eye open for any of the stuff seeping out of the cliffs or the drains.

The mile-long Barmouth Bridge, spanning the mouth of the Mawddach estuary plus a marshy area on the south bank, has a rich history of its own. It was opened by the Aberystwyth and Welsh Coast Railway in 1867, when it included a drawbridge section to allow the passage of tall ships. This was later replaced by a metal swing-bridge, but the rest of the viaduct's wooden construction was the source of its major problem, the timbers having severely weakened over time. By the 1980s, locomotives had been banned from crossing the bridge, immediately stopping any freight traffic and restricting passenger trains to diesel multiple units, which don't need a heavy locomotive to haul them. Various repairs finally prompted the reintroduction of locomotives and today Barmouth Bridge still forms part of the Cambrian Coast line, from Shrewsbury to Pwllheli, whose scenic route would run parallel to my own all the way from Porthmadog to Aberdovey and beyond.

The wooden walkway runs on the landward side of the viaduct and today was surprisingly busy, with pedestrians, dogs, cyclists and one moped. Though the views up the choppy, dark blue of the estuary and over the interlocking grey-green headlands up to misty Cadair Idris were eye-catching, no one stopped for long to admire them, hurried on by the chill east wind. A small picnic area at the southern end, though, lay in the shelter of a hillock and here I pulled over for some refreshment while reading the information boards. In crossing the bridge, I'd rejoined NCN 8, but from here it would shoot off in the wrong direction for my destination, Aberdovey: that is, it went eastwards along the Mawddach Trail towards Dolgellau, a route liberally spattered with Sites of Special Scientific Interest for the flora and fauna. John Ruskin believed the walk from Dolgellau to Barmouth to be the finest in the world – closely followed by that from Barmouth to Dolgellau. As for me, I happily set off again on the main road towards Fairbourne.

I'd already decided to make a short diversion to Fairbourne itself, a small holiday village created in the 1890s by Arthur McDougall, of self-raising flour fame. But it was neither the resort nor its tiny light railway that I'd come to look at. It was the 'Dragon's Teeth'. Cycling onto the prom, I couldn't miss them: arranged high on the beach, a set of tank traps designed to slow down any invasion from the Irish Sea that Hitler might have been contemplating. From the name 'Dragon's Teeth', I'd been expecting a few isolated, rusty spikes, but was surprised to see a whole row of tightly spaced concrete blocks, each about a cubic metre and spaced perhaps two metres apart. They ran from the cliffs that closed in the southern end of the beach as far as the eye could see to the north and must have been several hundred in number. Though exposed directly to erosion from the sea for over sixty years, they were almost all completely intact.

Reflecting – as I should more often than I do – that I'm one of Britain's lucky generation, I pushed off up the steep A493, squeezed between the steep hill out of which it had been hacked and the railway, beach and sea into which it threatened to crumble. At Llwyngwril, a village seemingly comprised almost entirely of converted chapels, I passed a school adorned by a large banner warning 'No School, No Village, No Future'. Rather an exaggeration, surely, but a catchy slogan nonetheless. At Rhoslefain, the obvious option was to follow the main road on its wiggly route around Broad Water, but I fancied the likelihood of a shortcut to Tywyn across the railway bridge that spans the mouth of the River Dysynni as it exits Broad Water into Cardigan Bay.

Two miles later I found myself staring at a barbed wire fence designed to persuade me that this was not a good idea. Should I still be tempted by the short climb over the bridge to the far bank, which seemed almost in touching distance, a large sign declared that such a venture would cost me £2,000. If only they'd spent the money that it cost for the fence and the sign on a mere thirty metres of path over the bridge instead.

Disgruntled, I scrunched back to the lane and followed it through some remote sheep pasture to the north of the river. A small lamb that had wandered too far along the road from its mother was so alarmed by my presence, even though I'd slowed down to a crawl, that it jumped in panic against the fence and bounced back upside down onto the tarmac. Just as I feared it had broken its neck, it pulled itself together and scampered behind me in search of safety.

The correct route was now obvious, even to me, and so I rejoined the main road at Bryncrug. Taking a short side-route, I found myself on a quiet lane that crossed the narrow-gauge Talyllyn Railway before meandering lazily through a patchwork of roughly fenced meadows. Nothing much seemed to be moving this late afternoon, except the raised walking stick of an elderly man on a bench, who called out as I pedalled by:

'Lovely day for it, boy!'

Joining the main road at what must have been the local rush hour, I had to keep a sharp eye on the traffic for a mile or two before pulling up on the coast side of the road at a stile giving access to the golf course that occupied the dunes between the road and the sea. Though not a golfer myself, even I could see that the sharp westerlies buffeting this scenic links course must offer the player a severe challenge – but a sign on the stile showed that the wind wasn't the only hazard: 'Cattle graze the course as a matter of right from 1 May to 31 October annually.'

Just a mile beyond the golf course, I swung into Aberdovey, passing a number of large, elegant mansions in the trees to my left. It was immediately obvious that here was a seaside town a cut above the rest. The cycling day ended as I pulled into a large car park with the sea on one side and our B&B on the other. Here I sat for a few minutes both to enjoy the view and reflect on the day.

Despite the odd mismatch between map and reality, it had, in truth, been another successful day for Sustrans. Their cycle routes had kept me segregated from the traffic where possible and offered me several alternatives to the coast road – even if one of them hadn't yet been built. When it had, I felt sure that I'd be back to try it, for the scenery at this north end of Cardigan Bay is different at every turn and the constant presence of the sea simply adds to the pleasure of being out of doors. With most of the west coast still to go, things were looking good.

Day 12

Nicer than Nice:
Aberdovey to Aberystwyth

Aberdovey is Godalming-on-Sea. Its south-facing site at the mouth of the overwhelmingly beautiful Dovey estuary gives it both sparkling sunrises and balmy sunsets – on those days when the sun shines, that is. The little harbour is always witness to some maritime activity, the broad, tide-washed sands stretch for miles, and, as I'd seen, it boasts an eighteen-hole golf links just around the corner. Almost all the houses, hotels, pubs and restaurants face the wide seascape and, with the sprinkling of a few mansions in the hills, the property prices are at Surrey stockbroker levels. As

I'd pedalled into town the previous evening, a shiny Rolls-Royce Corniche had pulled out in front of me and, from its guitar-related number plate and the word that he lived around here, a good bet was that it had been driven by Led Zeppelin's Robert Plant. The young English landlord of our B&B, the Seabreeze, couldn't afford to live here himself, he told us, and commuted in from Tywyn every day.

Both he and the morning were bright and breezy. His rendition of Sam Cooke's 'Cupid' came wafting in from the kitchen as Julie and I breakfasted by the bay window, observing Aberdovey's sand shovellers making a far more efficient job of it than their Barmouth counterparts. Delivering the toast, our landlord told us that every year 200 dumper trucks of sand are shifted from the growing beach in front of us out to the golf course. This morning the sand was blowing against the legs of an eastbound jogger and the face of her black spaniel. Neither seemed to care.

A relatively short day ahead allowed us time for a wander through the wonders of an Aberdovey morning. On the beach, still mostly untrampled, isolated pebbles had forced the fine, wind-blown sand into tiny, shaded valleys between slowly shifting ridges. Low wavelets battled against the breeze to sink into the sand, while out in the middle of the estuary, the local lifeboat was making stubborn headway along the choppy surface of the main channel out to sea, and presumably to someone's aid. Just upriver at the harbour, two early sailors were silhouetted against the risen sun as they discussed what possibilities the day might offer and, as we approached them, the sounds of flapping sails and banging ropes came to dominate even the persistent calls of the wheeling gulls. Back up near the road, in a small parking area, a forest of white masts rose from those craft still on trailers or propped on trestles. Behind the masts lay the multi-coloured row of shops and guest houses that forms the continuous, one-sided frontage to Aberdovey's main street.

Between the sixteenth and nineteenth centuries, Aberdovey had been a significant shipbuilding centre, some of the vessels built here even crossing the Atlantic. Tourists and rich local residents have clearly now taken over as the main source of income. Leaving Julie to boost the takings of the clothes shops, I set off eastwards, upriver towards a crossing point and into the teeth of the wind – though careless of it, for who could care for anything but the blue day?

The grandest of the town's houses seemed to spread along the banks of the estuary, both above and below the road. As this perfect spring morning was exactly what their millionaire owners had paid their money for, I hoped they'd scheduled today for Aberdovey rather than for the yacht anchored off Nice. Tightly slated walls and closely cropped hedges abutted the left of the road while, to the right, waving branches – most with early leaves, but some still bare – broke up the rippling milky reflections from the Dovey, which gradually narrowed the further I pedalled east, from sand-lined estuary to reed-lined river. Between the trees and the shore snaked the rusty rails of the Cambrian Coast Line, strangely quiet today, while beyond the river, high misty hills stretched back towards Plynlimon, the highest point in the Cambrian Mountains and some of whose waters drained to England, a land that now seemed impossibly far away.

Just after Aber-Tafol, where a few small boats rocked agitatedly in a small cove, the A493 turned inland and reluctantly I had to follow it. The landscape opened out into standard Mid-Wales fare: sheep, farms, sheep, hedges and sheep. Some daffodils were already over, daisies and violets taking on the wayside duties for a while.

Cruising in from Happy Valley on the left came NCN 8, having missed the glories of Aberdovey (a careless own goal, but I'd stopped scoring by now) and an unclassified road shot off to the right, where my map told me it would come within half a mile of another tempting railway bridge across the river, which would have saved me about ten miles. Having learned my lesson from yesterday's fruitless diversions, though, I plugged on, intending to pedal up to the station just beyond the bridge later in the day anyway.

At Pennal, NCN 8 and I had the same idea and we dived off the main road for a short parallel stint through the little hamlet of Llugwy. Here the woodland was dotted with large Victorian and Edwardian houses of the sort where Agatha Christie might have spent an afternoon in the window-seat admiring the view along the estuary and jotting down the plot for *The Murder of Roger Ackroyd*. (She didn't.) After swishing through a green, primrose-trimmed tunnel, I emerged once again on the dandelion-and-daisy main road.

The Dovey's lowest bridging point for road users finally arrived at Pen-y-bont, which Julie and I had crossed by car on our 'day off'. Just north of here, at Bron-Yr-Aur cottage, Robert Plant and Jimmy Page allegedly wrote and recorded part of Led Zep's third album, *Led Zeppelin III*, in 1970. At the time the band was the biggest-selling album act in the world, but they escaped here to the 1950s holiday retreat of the Plant family. The 'allegedly' is merely in recognition of another 'allegedly': that the cottage had no electricity (or running water). So how did they record anything? Whatever, Plant's association with the area is evidently nothing new.

Having toured Machynlleth a few days before (see Day 6), I stayed only long enough for a snack this time around and was soon on my way again. Leaving Mach, I also left NCN 8 definitively behind as my old friend and adversary headed south-east to Cardiff while I plunged south-westwards, down the opposite bank of the Dovey to that of this morning's ride and into Ceredigion, which, as Cardiganshire, was one of the original Phase 5 counties (those created by Edward I in the thirteenth century) before being swallowed by Dyfed for a few years. Named after local chieftain Ceredig, Ceredigion was originally a Phase 4 political unit, one of the small, squabbling fifth-century kingdoms.

For a while, the A487 kept within sight of the river meadows to the right, where a schoolboy soccer game was being played on a rugby pitch, the goalkeeper diving hopelessly for a ball way above his head but still below the crossbar. The features on my side of the road were less lively: a dead badger, a dead squirrel and a lay-by 'sausage stop' closed and up for sale. My immediate target was a railway station – and the satisfaction of a thirty-eight-year-old desire.

One September morning, as a young eighteen-year-old (younger, in truth, than most eighteen-year-olds), I'd packed all my possessions into two suitcases and boarded a train at a small East Midlands station, headed for three years at university in a town I'd never visited and could hardly pronounce: Aberystwyth. Travelling east–west by train in Britain was then, as now, a complicated affair and I'd already changed at Derby, Birmingham New Street and Wolverhampton High Level before a last change where the line splits to run either side of the Dovey estuary, at Dovey Junction. Here, I hauled my blue and brown cases out of the train yet again, but this station was rather different from the others. For one thing, the single island platform was full to the edges with young people of my own age, heading, I assumed, to the same destination. They had, however, stranger clothes than mine, untidier hair, unusual accents and unpredictable luggage – shaped like trumpets, guitars and goodness knows what else. For another, beyond the tracks lay no townscape, but a wilderness of waving reeds, lumpy green tussocks and winding rivulets, the like of which I'd never seen. The fifteen minutes or so I waited there, too shy to join in the conversations but avidly listening to them, made a great impression on me. Although I'd subsequently passed through Dovey Junction many times since that day, I'd never seen any means of access other than the railway tracks and, to be honest, had no clear idea of where it actually was. Today I intended to put that right, as my map showed the station barely half a mile off the road and accessible by a path I'd never noticed from the window and parallel to the Aber line. (Around here, 'Aber' = Aberystwyth.)

Five miles out of Mach and there it was: a big 'Dovey Junction' sign for the odd passenger in a thousand who wanted to reach the station from the road. I pulled off, turned down the track – and immediately reversed back up again as a truck trundled up the narrow lane towards me. As it reached the road, the driver leaned out of his window.

'Hopin' to catch a train?'

'No, I'm just going to look at the station.'

'No you're not. It's possessed.'

This was possibly the last thing I'd expected him to say. He didn't look as though he was fleeing a railway ghost. He saw my confusion.

'I mean there's a possession on. By the contractors raising the platform and stuff. The line's closed.'

This explained the morning's lack of trains.

'Oh, can I just walk down the track to take a look?'

'No.'

'Not just a little bit?'

'No. They won't let you in.'

With that, I gave up and let him flee the possession. If I'd have arrived five minutes before I'd have gone down the track unimpeded anyway, as no sign gave any indication either that trains were not running or that the station was closed. I walked over to the notice board, where, half-hidden behind a list of candidates for an upcoming election and a photograph of one of them, an A4 sheet in closely typed script advised me that £13 million was being spent to improve the Cambrian Line and reduce the risk of... and there the balding head of the would-be councillor took over. Risk of flooding, I would guess. Fair enough. Seeing Dovey Junction from outside the station would have to wait another thirty-eight years.

Despite Cardigan Bay's scenic splendours, it was proving strangely frustrating. First Machynlleth's empty museum, then Shell Island's ford and the missing cycle track, then the fenced-off bridge and now the inaccessible station: ever since Porthmadog my route had been littered with failed plans. So it was with some apprehension that I approached Furnace, site of an eighteenth-century iron foundry and modern-day museum. Closed for renovations of course. Not only closed but dramatically fenced off to deter me from even touching its walls, though not preventing my admiration of the half-restored, giant mill wheel and the gushingly unstoppable waterfall next door.

At tiny Tre'r-ddôl I pulled into a cafe declaring 'Joe's – everything else is just ice cream', ordered something else and it turned out to be a cup of coffee. The lady assistant, who listened kindly to my few, poor Welsh phrases, recommended 'the flat route' to Aber favoured by her cycling husband, via Llanbadarn Fawr, but I was already on familiar ground and had a small diversion planned at the top of the hill anyway.

With the scent of the beach already in my nostrils, I whooshed through Bow Street, thought to have been named after the London street in the 1770s because of the 'bow' in the road alignment here. A more recent oddity of Bow Street's is that in 2006 a tornado blew material from here as far as Corris, twenty miles to the north.

Forming my own little wind system, I crested the brow at Waun Fawr to glimpse the jagged skyline of Aber promenade before turning left into the university campus and illegally zigzagging down the one-ways to inspect the Geography department's building, which, alas, looked as though it hadn't been painted since I'd studied there 35 years before. The afternoon was warm enough to have brought a gaggle of students out onto the grass, where they sprawled around just as we'd done... and from what I could gather, were also solving the world's problems with the same solutions that we'd proposed – and conspicuously failed to implement.

A story in the local paper, the *Cambrian News* (established 1860), revealed another way of trying to get on. An Aber student, doing a master's degree in computer science, had recently been convicted of money laundering. The scheme involved a scam whereby people in the US who happened to have the same name as the villain had been duped into forwarding him some money. His name was Salami and it seems that the scheme was not notably successful, since the judge waived the fine on the grounds that Salami had no money at all – not a sausage.

Having temporarily satisfied my nostalgia without dragging Julie down memory lane, I freewheeled down the hill to join her on the prom at the Belle Vue Royal. This, Aber's premier seafront hotel, would have been a bit too 'premier' for me – being as proud to be tight as the 'Cardis' (Cardiganshire locals) are rumoured to be among the Welsh – if it weren't for the fact that we were not alone. By a miracle of logistics, our schedule had been moulded to coincide with that most self-indulgent of events: a university reunion.

This wasn't an official reunion, although rumour has it that these exist, with their gowns, top tables and even former lecturers. No, this was just a bunch of student friends, including Rhodri, whom we'd already encountered at Lland'od. The connection was our hall of residence – a sea-front spot with ice-cream views – and we've met every four years or so since... well, since some of us were still about twelve, judging from the photographs.

The traditional showing of old photos comes somewhere between the traditional walk over Constitution Hill, the traditional 'kicking the bar' and the traditional handing over of the contacts file to the next organiser. Constitution Hill is a 150-metre outcrop at the northern end of the town's promenade, access to the top of which can be achieved via an 1896 funicular railway – but which we intend to keep climbing on foot until forced into the 'old folks' railway'. 'Kicking the bar' is a tradition more easily described than explained. People walking to this same end of the prom simply touch the railing at the end once with each foot before turning around to walk back. It's said to have been going on for a century or more. Among the explanations I've heard are that locals do it to distinguish themselves from visitors; that superstitious students do it to guarantee their degree (and do it with both feet at once to get a first!); and, more prosaically, that male students used to do it just to pass the time while waiting for female students from Alexandra Hall, for many years a women-only hall of residence.

With partners nowadays invited to our reunions as well, this year saw a first-timer, who, on witnessing all these traditions, suggested that we needed a shake-up and therefore volunteered to organise the next reunion in Paris. Paris? Paris??!! Have you gone raving mad?

As we all sauntered along the prom after our own 'formal' meal, trying to remember whether ties should have been compulsory at the meal and what the names of the demolished cinemas used to be, about half a dozen semi-naked young students burst out of Terrace Road, skittered across the prom and the pebbles, shrieked into the steel-grey sea, panted back up the beach and shivered, barefoot, across the road and out of sight. I think they were all male, but then my eyesight is going the same way as my memory. This prompted some recollections of a more regrettable university tradition: the initiation ceremony, circa 1970.

We victims (all the hall's freshers) had been told to line up after dinner on the cafeteria stairs wearing just our swimming trunks. One by one, those ahead of me were led around the corner to the back yard, from where screams, splashes and 'Yeaarrrrgh!'s rent the chill November air. My turn around the corner revealed a tin bath full of what looked like yesterday's leftovers mixed with fertilizer and salad cream. I subsequently discovered it was actually mayonnaise, but otherwise I was spot on.

Having been totally (totally) immersed in the frigid concoction, we were led, still barefoot and surely looking like the survivors of a sixteenth-century culinary eruption in Franz Josef Land, to the pebble beach opposite, where it was made gleefully clear to us that the hall's showers would be out of bounds to freshers until at least 11 p.m. and that the lurching black rollers of the Irish Sea constituted our only hope of toiletry improvement until after the next indignity. Already frozen to – and beyond – the bone, I joined my miserable colleagues in the breakers. Thankfully, my memory cells must have been frozen by the shock, as I have no further recollection until surfacing, as directed, in the lower Marine Bar with a pint of Worthington 'E' in front of me.

Then there was some game. I think it required an intimate knowledge of the Llanelli front row, Tom and Jerry or Vivaldi's *Four Seasons* (rum folk, the Welsh, I remember thinking). My general knowledge having been found wanting, I was coerced into drinking several pints of 'E' down in one, having previously managed only half a pint down in thirty minutes. The number eleven seems to echo through the years, but eleven pints would surely have seen me out for the count until about 1976. Whatever, I was ill, I was filthy, I was apparently initiated and was thereafter on constant alert for subsequent attacks from the Forciau Outerspaciau Cymraeg (the Alien Forces of Wales).

Nearly forty years on, all of us who'd suffered this ordeal could still recall the icy chill of the waves. And here's the rub: a good many of us then proceeded to inflict exactly the same indignities on the following year's freshers. Maybe it's us that were raving mad.

Day 13

Sausages, Chips and Honey Ice Cream: Aberystwyth to New Quay

After the reunion had provided a day or two's much needed break from pedalling – and, for Julie, a much-needed opportunity to talk with someone other than me – we were off again, on a dull but warm morning. I just had time before leaving Aber to indulge in a leisurely spin along the front, all the way from the north bar, the one that is ritually kicked, to the south bar, the one beyond the harbour where I understand kicking is optional. Eagle-eyed for any changes in the last four years, I saw barely any – indeed barely any in the last forty years.

Aberystwyth is four towns for the price of one. At one level it's another standard Mid-Wales town: Edward I castle built in Phase 5 (thirteenth-century Norman suppression), captured by Glyndŵr in Phase 6 (fifteenth-century Welsh rebellion), charter granted in Phase 7 (sixteenth-century political union) and market town thereafter. Even for a ruin, the castle is a bit of a ruin, having been destroyed by the Parliamentarians in the Civil War.

It's also a classic Phase 8, Victorian resort: arrival of the railway, new-fangled holidays, seaside location, taking the air... At one point, Aberystwyth was even marketed as 'the Biarritz of Wales'. What's special about Aber in this respect is its almost perfectly preserved rows of former hotels along the promenade. What's odd, though, is that the most impressive of these, the Castle Hotel, never actually opened, its owner having gone bankrupt and the building having been sold to become the main building of the University College of Wales in 1872.

And so the third is the university town. A great many of the shops, bars and other businesses are very obviously primed to service the 12,000 students – about as many as there are other residents. The former sea-front hotels now mostly provide student accommodation and the Penglais Campus dominates the hill behind the town. During the reunion, five of us had wandered into the old Main College building on the front, still used for administration, and, with no one around, started peering into all the rooms... until a noise and a stern 'Who's there?' saw us doing a quick runner: bank manager, musician, magistrate, technologist and writer – pillars of society, all scampering out of a side door like guilty teenagers.

The fourth face of Aber is an administrative one. Plonked more or less in the middle of Wales, its location has for many years been preferred to Cardiff by a good number of national institutions, including the National Library of Wales, one of the small number of libraries entitled to a free copy of every book published in the UK – including the one you are reading. With this and the university, it's often claimed that Aber must be home to more books per head of population than any other town in the world – including Hay-on-Wye.

It's also home to the Ceredigion Museum and four of us had called in here the previous day, not because its marketing blurb quotes a description of it having 'one of the most beautiful museum interiors in Britain' (www.ceredigion. gov.uk), but because in our student days it had not been a museum at all but the splendid Coliseum Cinema, with its once-plush seats, its single 100-watt light bulb in place of the central grand chandelier and, once this had been suddenly extinguished, its corny, one-fingered organ tune that introduced racy classics of the era, such as *Prudence and the Pill* or *The Virgin Soldiers*. The museum's talkative assistant – or perhaps curator – was extremely knowledgeable on the history of the 1904 building and told us that it was in 1977, just after a showing of *Raid on Entebbe* and then *Bambi* (an interesting programme) that the Coliseum had finally closed, to emerge five years later as this museum. He was also able to reveal an interesting snippet not to be found in any of the official marketing material: that the 'beautiful museum' quote is in fact from a remark made by Judith Iscariot – or rather the actress who played Judith in *Monty Python's Life of Brian*, Aberystwyth resident Sue Jones-Davies. (Soon after this visit, she became Mayor of Aberystwyth, successfully overturned the town's amazing thirty-year ban on the film and, at the time of writing, was due to host a charity screening, at which a number of Monty Python stalwarts were expected as guests.)

Having swung round the harbour, which still sheltered the odd fishing boat but was dominated by pleasure craft, and past the world's best chip shop, Greasy Annie's (not the cafe's real name), I cruised over the river bridge. Despite the town's name, this is the mouth of the River Rheidol, the Ystwyth entering the sea a few hundred metres further south. Up on my right loomed the familiar outline of Pen Dinas, apparently a hill with a chimney, but in fact a hill topped by an Iron-Age fort and a chimney-shaped monument to the Duke of Wellington.

Exactly a mile out of town sits a rather remarkable milestone that bears an impressive eighteen destinations, including London (210 miles) and – my target for lunch – Aberaeron (fifteen).

After several other routes split off to the east, following river valleys inland, the Aberaeron road mounted a steep incline and I soon found myself walking through Chancery. This was the location of the Conrah Hotel, the sumptuous scene for reunion dinners in years past, but now out of bounds as we'd been told we were too numerous (or perhaps too noisy). What I didn't know when we used to eat here was that this Victorian mansion was once the home of the Smith's Crisps heiress – maybe this is where all those little blue salt bags went.

The scenery had quickly become rural again: a slow, brown fox ambled by a noisy brook to the left, while to the right gorse bushes threw bright yellow patches over the sheep pasture, beyond which, popping in and out of view, stretched the dull blue of Cardigan Bay. And then somewhere between Chancery and Llanrhystud, I suddenly squeezed on the brakes, having almost passed an extraordinary sight before realising its significance. Behind a low hedge on the right stood a field. A very unusual field, for where the sheep or cattle should have been was... soil! After thirteen days and over 300 miles of pedalling, I'd passed my very first arable field in Wales. I saluted it.

Ways down to the beach are few and far between here and it wasn't until Llanon that I turned off, past a patchwork of well-tended front gardens and down to a banked beach formed of smooth, grey pebbles at Llansantffraed. The *Encyclopaedia* remarks on an unusual land ownership pattern behind the beach, but makes no mention of the weird sight right on it. At the northern end of the beach, meandering languidly into the sea, was the little River Peris, immediately beyond which – and forming its right bank – was what looked like a giant cake: four metres of pebbly white cliff topped by a thin grass icing. What was so bizarre was that the cliff had all the appearance of having been freshly cut that morning – and the fact that it's not marked on the map as The Devil's Wedding Cake, as it surely would have been in times gone by, suggests that this tiny river had indeed eroded it very recently and very neatly. Why? I've no idea.

By the time I'd puzzled over and failed to resolve this mystery, the sun had come out and shone over the green fields that sloped down to the sea all the way to Aberaeron. Without Tetley I might have set off along the beach, but back to the A487 it was and up a steep hill where the good old sheep once again shared my view – this time back over Llanon and over a large caravan site beyond, as far as Constitution Hill in Aber.

At the crest of my hill I was pleased to see a 'sausage stop' ahead: the Happy Chomper, parked in a lay-by and drawing a queue of would-be chompers. I joined them for my lunch's first course and, while chomping down my sausage sandwich, was joined by the proprietor, popping outside for a quick cigarette break. With the weather improving, he was in an expansive mood. Having moved to Aberaeron from Wolverhampton just a few years back, he already knew he'd never regret it, he told me. The Happy Chomper calendar seemed to be full: in this lay-by, with its panoramic sea view, Monday to Friday; at a local football match on Saturday; and at a motor event on Sunday. Being confident he'd be bringing home the bacon for some time yet – and, with Wolves having won three-nil the previous night – you could say the Chomper was chipper. And his mood rubbed off on me as I winged down the hill, in the opposite direction to a tiny black Austin Seven, circa 1931, driven by an elderly lady complete with hat, coat, fox stole and horn-rimmed glasses, and doing all of fifteen miles an hour. Welcome to Aberaeron.

If you've never been here, you can easily get a good idea of it by nipping down to your local DIY store and standing in front of the coloured paint shelves. Squint your eyes: that's what Aberaeron looks like. I've been to a few places with the odd row of brightly painted houses – Portree and Tobermory spring to mind – but Aberaeron's in a different league. As far as I could see, the front of every single house – and of a good many commercial enterprises too – was painted in some colour you wouldn't normally associate with masonry. This year's specialities seemed to be Cranberry Purple and Arriva Trains Turquoise. Distinctly odd on their own, but quite arresting as part of an entire townscape that resembled nothing less than a giant child's colouring book.

My objective for dessert was not far from the Harbourmaster Hotel (in Kingfisher Blue) and had a queue even longer than the Happy Chomper's... but, as always, the Hive on the Quay's honey ice cream was well worth the wait. Sitting on a bench by the neat little harbour, I fell into conversation with another Hive customer.

'Oh, I once had a bike,' he revealed in an Essex accent, although he hailed from Suffolk. 'One o' those little foldin' jobs. Raleigh, I fink.'

'Moulton, possibly,' I suggested.

'Yeah, Raleigh,' he went on, licking his ice cream from time to time. 'Well, I knew sumink was wrong as soon as I folded it and couldn't... (Lick)... couldn't get the bugger unfolded again. The widget on this bit didn't match the widget on that bit. I 'eld the fing in the air – I was younger in them days – put my eye along it – better eye an' all – an' guess what?'

'What?'

'It was bent, that's what. (Lick.) Paid good money for it an' I gotta bent bike. So what d'you fink I did?'

'Took it back?'

'Pah! Took it back! D'you 'ear that, Ethel?' Whether Ethel heard or not, she didn't reveal. ''E don't know me, does 'e? Nah, I took me 'ammer to it – wrapped in a greasy cloth o' course (Lick) – and give it a few whacks on the bottom bracket an' then...'

After a detailed, blow-by-blow account of his refashioning of the bike, the Suffolk cyclist approached the climax of his tale.

'So, I sets the bike back on the floor an' nah the bloody fing won't even move – wheels won't go round at all. So what d'you fink I did?'

'Threw it away?'

'Nah, I took it back, didn't I? Took it to the shop, showed 'em it didn't work – an' guess what they said?'

'That you'd modified the bike and couldn't have your money back?'

He looked at me, surprised. 'Yeah. You don't work for Raleigh, do you?'

I confirmed I did not.

'Anyway,' said the Suffolk cyclist, standing up, 'this ice cream's not bad, is it? (Lick.) See ya.'

The hill out of Aberaeron was even steeper than that coming in and, perhaps weighed down by sausage and ice cream, I trudged up it pretty slowly, past the new county offices of Ceredigion. With a population of just 1,500, Aberaeron is a new addition to the long series of tiny Welsh county towns, past and present.

It was only another seven miles or so to New Quay, the overnight stop, along another stretch where the cliffs rendered the shore mostly inaccessible and where there was little else of interest. Having never visited the place, though, I was looking forward to New Quay and met up with Julie at what turned out to be her highest-rated B&B of the trip. Run by an Anglo-Dutch couple, the Craig-Y-Wig Guest House, a few minutes walk from the sea front, was immaculately presented, from the spotless bathroom, with its 'Beam me up, Scotty' shower cubicle, to the chocolates on the coffee tray, everything was just perfect. And one of our least expensive stopovers, to boot. Walking down to the harbour, Julie asked:

'Why don't we book in for next year right now?'

'I haven't even seen New Quay yet.'

'I have. While you've been dawdling on your bike, I've been scouting around – and it's got it all: views, walks, beaches…'

'Pubs?'

'Pubs. Even country pubs inland, from what I could see on my little tour. And other little coves just down the coast for a change of scene. In fact, it's like a kind of Cornwall that nobody knows is here.'

We'd walked as far as the harbour. New Quay is sheltered from the prevailing westerlies by the crook of the coast, with the extra help of the 'new' quay, which turns out to be 300 years old. It's yet another old port and shipbuilding town economically saved by tourism. Though there's still some fishing for lobster and crab, it was evident from a glance at the harbour that sailing for pleasure has now taken over.

'Let's try the pubs tonight first,' I suggested.

The Wellington Inn (the Duke must have had a big West Wales fan club) served up a very steamy curry and some free entertainment from the next table, in the form of a little girl who insisted – despite the best efforts of her parents – in practising very loudly the new words she'd learned: 'Money Money. Fissnchip. Dink Dink. Drunk Drunk. Row Row Row the Boat...' In fifteen years' time, the words probably won't have changed much.

After our own 'dink dinks', we resolved to look at next year's calendar when we got home and slept soundly with the help of another of the Craig-Y-Wig's star attractions: the trip's most luxurious, most comfortable bed.

Day 14

Diesels and Coracles: New Quay to Eglwyswrw

Breakfast conversation in a British guest house is traditionally restricted to a companionable 'Good morning' and a brief comment on the weather, but, having been joined at our table the next morning by a friendly couple on a three-day tour from South Wales, we formed an unusually talkative bunch. The conversation turned again to Welsh naming conventions. One of our fellow residents had grown up in the Valleys and started reminiscing.

'Well, our local chiropodist was Pete the Feet,' he told us, 'and then I remember two twins, Ron and Rob, who grew up to be Ron the Bus and – this is true, mind – Rob the Bank.'

'I thought nicknames were supposed to come from the surnames,' I said.

'Ah yes,' he conceded. 'Them too. There was a boxer born down our street who lost half his ear in fight. Know what they called 'im?'

'No.'

'Jones Eighteen Months.'

'Why?'

'It's a year and an 'alf, innit?'

Wondering if I could make money as a straight man, I wiped the marmalade from my beard and we eventually bid our new-found friends farewell.

It had rained heavily overnight and, with dark clouds still rolling in from the west, I was already wrapped up in waterproofs as I pushed up the steep, south-western route out of town. New Quay is tiny and I soon found myself riding – or more often walking – between sodden fields and under dripping trees. My route crossed a series of narrow valleys, whose streams tumbled noisily left to right and down to the sea. In the gloom a bright yellow house stood out in one hamlet, shortly followed by a giant corrugated shed that seemed to be acting as a warehouse for empty cardboard boxes. At the village of Llwyndafydd, so many roads radiated from the leafy site of its pub that I leaned Tetley against the many-fingered signpost to study the map, in a rare shaft of sunlight. I was aiming for Cenarth, about fifteen miles away on the River Teifi, but, with no clear route there, plumped for the yellow road to Plwmp – for no better reason that I liked the name: I think we all know the road to Plwmp, don't we?

On arrival I was satisfied to note that there was still a 'Plwmp Post Office' and here, not knowing where the next snack opportunity might arise, I stocked up with a Twix and a Boost. With the next few miles along the A487 devoid not only of chocolate bars but also of much interest, I found myself obliged to keep shifting position in the saddle to prevent my nether regions from falling asleep – this may mean nothing to lady cyclists but should sound familiar to any chap that has cycled too long without a break. The many years when I would ride my bike with no padding at all in the trouser region do not bear thinking about. The Seventh Law of Cycle Touring is, of course:

A padded groin is a happy groin.

Somewhere near Tan-y-groes, heavy drops of rain began to pierce my helmet just as an intriguing brown tourist sign announced 'Internal Fire 200 metres' and pointed down a lane to the left. Without much thought other than of somewhere dry, I duly diverted, pulled into the small collection of sheds indicated by the sign and quickly garaged Tetley and myself under a canopy and out of the strengthening downpour.

After I'd disengaged myself from my dripping equipment, a breezy Irish woman beckoned me into what I was pleased to see was a small cafe, quite empty of customers but surrounded by the noise of invisible machines. As she served me coffee and ginger cake (excellent), it was clear that she assumed I already appreciated the subject of the museum

– which I was too embarrassed to admit that I did not. Little by little, however, it became clear that the 'Internal Fire' in question was neither a metaphor for human determination nor the after-effects of a fiery vindaloo but marketing-speak for the internal combustion engine – and further, that the historical hero to which this out-of-the-way little museum was dedicated was Herr Rudolf Diesel, inventor of the engine that bears his name. My guide was especially fired up herself this year, as it was the 150th anniversary of Diesel's birth, and she'd fired me up enough to buy an entrance ticket.

As I swung open a sturdy door, the noise of the engines intensified and I found myself alone in a long, low, green room lined with elderly but shiny machinery, relentlessly thrusting pistons and not a few oily rags. Now, I'm not actually the best person to profit from this kind of opportunity. For a start, I've never understood – and probably never will understand – how any engine, internal or external, fired by diesel, coal or human waste, actually works... and it seemed from the explanatory notices that such a basic failing in any visitor had not been anticipated. However, I was determined to find something diverting to justify my investment and did so by studying the original documentation that accompanied each machine. My favourite was the Troubleshooting Guide for the 1936 'Petter' Diesel Engine, which advised the user what action to take if the engine knocks, if it races or if it hunts. I hadn't even known that diesel engines went racing and hunting.

After what I judged to be a respectful time, I returned to the relative calm of the cafe, where the Irish lady assured herself that I'd enjoyed my visit, assured me that I wouldn't be the day's only visitor and assured us both that the weather was definitely clearing. Despite – or perhaps because of – the museum's rather specialist collection, I offer to all slightly tired cyclists the Eighth Law of Cycle Touring:

Be diverted.

In fact, my next call was another diversion, albeit a planned one, and another museum.

If I understand it correctly, it is Cenarth's location on the beautiful River Teifi, where coracle building has been practised for generations, that explains its hosting of the National Coracle Centre. A coracle, explained the jolly Welsh woman, the museum's only attendant, to the sweaty cyclist, its only visitor, is a simple river craft: basically a basket with a seat. A big, round-bottomed basket and a basket covered in animal hide and sealed with lanolin, but a basket nevertheless, fashioned from willow and hazel. Having encouraged me to try out a sample seat for size and stressed that I could spend as much time as I wished, she withdrew, leaving me alone in a space about the size of a large living room, and wondering whether I could spin out here even as much time as I'd recently passed gazing at the industrial invention of Mr Diesel.

While there's little more that can be said about the nature of the craft itself, there was actually a great deal to learn about where, when and to what purpose the coracle has been put over the years. For a start, it's not just Welsh. There were photographs, drawings and descriptions that revealed coracles bobbing about in Scotland, Ireland, North America, the Middle East and Tibet. My favourite photo was of four well-dressed high-fliers from the British Embassy in Baghdad standing confidently in a coracle in the middle of what must have been the Tigris in, I think, the 1930s. It was, the attendant told me afterwards, one of the very ladies pictured there that brought the photo to the museum.

My favourite story, however, was of a local man of some resolve named Bernard Thomas and sometimes known as the 'coracle king'. In the 1970s, with a friend and their faithful coracle, Thomas set off to London, where they first gate-crashed the Boat Race (moved on by the police); then paddled around in the Trafalgar Square fountains (moved on by the police again); then, near Dover, pointed their craft at Calais (pushed back by a force-seven gale); then, when the weather abated, actually made it to the very edge of France (not allowed to land by the French authorities); and finally did cross the Channel and successfully land the coracle in France. The crossing took over thirteen hours.

About three weeks before my visit, BBC Wales reported that Thomas would finally give up fishing the Teifi in his coracle at the end of the season. He was eighty-five years old and had been paddling the river for eighty-one of those.

Just a stone's throw from the museum I'd spotted a cafe on the main road whose window display promised a decent cake selection within and there I accepted the young assistant's recommendation of a gooey, home-made concoction that required cutlery to tackle it and did the job of filling a cyclist's stomach very proficiently, but whose Welsh name I can't recall.

Although the ideal spot for the next overnight would have been Newport, this Pembrokeshire coastal town appeared to the casual Internet surfer to boast no accommodation at all and so I was due to meet up with Julie at a small B&B five miles inland at Eglwyswrw, a village whose name had proved so difficult for either of us that it had been anglicised to 'Iggly-Wiggly'.

The afternoon's route from Cenarth to Iggly-Wiggly was in fact much less wiggly than the morning's: a direct westward haul along the B4332, up out of the Teifi Valley, down and up the valleys of various left-bank tributaries and almost to the foot of the Preseli Hills. The morning's showers had passed, leaving a clear afternoon to show off the views in this little corner of Wales where the counties of Ceredigion, Carmarthenshire and Pembrokeshire compete for villages. It was rolling sheep territory (the territory, not the sheep, doing the rolling), with patches of anemones in small stands of mixed woodland, cowslips dotting the roadside and the smell of wild garlic hovering over the valleys. Traffic was sparse until I breezed into Iggly-Wiggly, an anonymous Pembrokeshire village on the busy A487, the main road that had charged down from Plwmp while I'd been on my little diesel-and-coracle diversion.

At the Postgwyn Guest House I was welcomed by Julie, by the friendly, middle-aged couple who ran it and, on the table of their cosy lounge, by an item I'd been looking out for ever since Monmouth: a slice of bara brith. Literally meaning 'speckled bread', bara brith had, I am ashamed to say, never passed my lips on any visit to Wales. On close examination, this 'bread' looked like simple fruit cake. On hesitant nibble, it tasted like simple fruit cake. On further gobble, it proved to be a very excellent fruit cake indeed.

Even though I was in danger of becoming caked out, after my third of the day, the talk turned to more food, and the nearest decent place to eat, our hosts suggested, was in Newport – and so, for the first time in the trip, Julie and I drove to dinner. Unsurprisingly, this pleasant enough little town, set a mile from the sea, did seem to have the odd place to sleep after all.

The Royal Oak was abuzz with laughter, both from the chaps at the bar and from a table accommodating ten ladies of a certain age who could only have been the WI. The Argentinian barmaid's English was slightly better than that of the Slovakian waitress, who was also, we discovered, her flatmate. On arrival in Wales, they'd found that, with neither speaking the other's native language, an English dictionary had to be constantly on hand for them to communicate at all. It was pretty entertaining not only to listen to the frantic – and mostly verb-free – messages passing between them about food orders...

'Puddinks table fife.'

'Escallop in bar.'

'Table three beell.'

... but also to the Argentinian dealing with bar orders in Welsh. Alas, this entertainment was short-lived, for when our own order arrived we were mysteriously removed from our ringside seat and ushered upstairs to consume it in a deserted and rather dreary restaurant. This banishment was, Julie informed me, the fault neither of an Argentinian barmaid nor of a Slovakian waitress but of an English cyclist whose own communication skills were woefully poor.

Day 15

Eggy Bolton and a Small Dispute: Eglwyswrw to St David's

With weather systems regularly rolling in from the nearby Atlantic, many mornings in south-west Wales must start with a peek around the bedroom curtain and the comment: 'Looks like a change in the weather.' This was one of those mornings. A thin mist had closed in and, though it wasn't actually raining at breakfast, the chances were that it would be once again by elevenses.

Collecting Tetley from the little shed that had housed him overnight, I asked our host about the B&B trade away from the coastal resorts.

'Trade's not bad', he said, 'but we're off anyway.'

'Off where?'

'Not far. Just to Newport. Nearer the golf course, you see. This place is up for sale.'

It turns out it had been on the market for some time: a 200-year-old cottage on a main road, with an extension and some land – I was surprised it hadn't gone quickly, but the 'credit crunch' evidently had knock-on effects far and wide. In the meantime, golf would still have to compete with business.

Semi-togged-up for the inevitable rain, I left Iggly-Wiggly westbound along the A487 for a while before turning south on a minor road and up a sudden hill of G3 gradient, sidestepping another dead badger that must have been unlucky to catch a passing car on this quiet lane. This was a controversial time for badgers and Pembrokeshire was at the heart of it.

Bovine tuberculosis (TB) is a serious disease in cattle caused by a bacterium of which they are natural hosts but which can infect nearly all warm-blooded animals. In Wales, in 2008, the number of cattle killed because of TB had risen from less than 700 a year (ten years previously) to nearly 8,000. Badgers definitely carry the TB bacterium too, but there's much debate about their role in transmitting it to cattle. Under a government-sponsored trial, 11,000 badgers had been culled in Britain and only three weeks before this misty day it had been announced that another cull would be undertaken in Pembrokeshire, an unfortunate hotspot for bovine TB – even though the value of any culling of badgers had been widely questioned.

Turning a corner just beyond the car-killed badger, I pulled up as a small number of cattle were being herded along the road ahead of me. Unusually, just one young man without a dog was in charge and, from a position behind the lumbering beasts, his method of diverting the front-lumberers into a field was one I hadn't seen before: he simply threw small stones at them. It seemed to work and they appeared quite unperturbed.

After a few more twists and turns on the exposed hilltops, I descended into the leafy valley of Cwm Gwaun – and there was immediately transported into a different world. This cleft in the hills, through which the youthful River Gwaun first trickles and then rushes, was narrow enough for the densely wooded sides to feel that morning like the tall, green walls of a long, winding room, whose ceiling was the dense cloud of mist above and whose floor was another sheet of grey mist rising from the river. Almost totally enclosed, the valley echoed loudly to birdsong but was so wet that no smells could be distinguished at all. With its gradual downhill gradient, but barely a vehicle to be seen, Cwm Gwaun formed an ideal cycling route – and indeed is designated by Sustrans as part of NCN 82.

The idyll ended abruptly with a short but extremely steep hill, on which the heel of my front foot just struggled past the toe of my back foot, making it a definite G4. Having emerged, panting, onto the B4313, I leaned Tetley against a signpost just as a well-used white van screeched to a halt, its driver winding down the window and calling out to me in a Birmingham accent.

'Oy, mite, do you know where I am?'

I pointed at the sign behind me, which revealed that we were three miles from Abergwaun ('mouth of the River Gwaun') – or Fishguard.

'Oh yeah, roight.'

Still with the window down, Brummie tapped a few numbers into his mobile, asked for someone called Michael and then embarked on a conversation that was probably as bemusing to overhear from the other end as it was from this.

'Moik! Roight, I've just come up an 'ill I couldn't get up and I'm three miles from Fishguard at a… (he looked over at the sign)… at a place with a Welsh name. Where are you? Eggy Bolton? Where's that? I'm not on the A40, I'm on… (I called it out to him)… on the B4313. (Pause…) No, Fishguard. Yes, Wiles! Where's Eggy Bolton? Well, it sounds loik Eggy Bolton to me, Moik.'

I handed him my map, which he took as though he'd never seen such a thing. I noticed there was no sat-nav in his vehicle either and wondered how he'd found his way here from the West Midlands.

'This bloke on a boik's jus' given me, loik, a map. O' course it's of Wiles, Moik. I told you: I'm three miles from Fishguard. Where are you? Yeah. Yeah. Well, why didn't you say so in the first plice, you plonker?'

Brummie pressed his red button and handed me the map.

'Thanks, mite. 'E's in Fishguard. Down 'ere intit?'

'Yes, bottom of the hill. Can't miss it. Er, what was that about Eggy Bolton?'

'Some Welsh name. Moik's Irish. I knew it'd be trouble.'

And with that he hurtled off. Looking at my map I couldn't find any kind of Bolton around here at all, Eggy or otherwise.

My lunchtime target was not egg but cheese, in the form of a Cheese Centre at Llangloffan, a fair way to the west. My route skirted Fishguard and took me instead through the hamlet of Bengal and along a short stretch of the busy A40, where, coincidentally, Julie's Golden Toyota overtook me with a wave and what she later told me was a puzzled look, since I was heading in completely the wrong direction. I'll admit to you now that at this point I was… if not exactly lost (for chaps with maps never quite descend to that level, do we?), then temporarily disorientated. The awkward folds of my various OS maps, together with some heavy drops of rain thereon, had conspired to send me slightly off beam and, taking advantage of a railway bridge for shelter, I shook the maps out, refolded them and pointed myself back in the right direction.

So, when I eventually arrived at the deserted village of Llangloffan and stood in front of the farm building where my map (the very latest OS edition) declared there was a Cheese Centre, I was astounded to see no sign of cheese at all, just a sign of recent metal construction declaring: 'Private. No Entry'.

Hmm.

I recalled The Geographer's Law of Reality, which, if it really existed, would state:

> Where map and reality diverge, it is always reality
> that is at fault.

I peered beyond the sign and through the drizzle, expecting to see, in the kitchen window, a group of geographers tucking into huge slabs of Pembrokeshire Cheddar. Nothing. No one. Reluctantly, I consulted the map with renewed suspicion and picked on the village of Mathry, some two miles to the west, where the magic letters PH should indicate a public house – but which, I now feared, may just as easily indicate a pet hamster or a Peruvian hatshop. Missing cycle tracks and now missing cheese centres: the Ordnance Survey had plummeted in my estimation.

Mathry turned out to exist all right, though. It's an attractive hill-top town and allegedly the birthplace of one Jemima Nicholas, who in 1797, armed with a sturdy pitchfork, single-handedly rounded up and detained a dozen of the 1,400 French invaders who formed part of the last invasion of Britain, from four warships moored off a nearby beach. They were already drunk and their leaders eventually signed the French surrender at the Royal Oak in Fishguard. Mathry's own PH, the Farmer's Arms, also existed and there I surrendered to a bowl of soup while my wet cycling gear dripped steadily onto their carpet.

It was a warm and friendly pub, with walls so thick that I didn't notice the drizzle had turned to rain until I was once again togged up and outside. Although I toyed with the attractive idea of an immediate return inside, a de-tog and an extended lunch of beer and sandwiches, I really wanted to pull in Wales's westernmost point that afternoon, doubling back to our scheduled overnight in St David's ready for an eastward surge the next day.

Less than a mile down the main road westward, I realised that any exposed headland would be a very silly idea indeed, for the rain had turned wetter (if that's possible) and switched to horizontal, carried by a stiff westerly straight into my eyes. At the tiny hamlet of Square and Compass (an unusual case of a village being named after its pub, rather than the other way round), I retreated into a bus shelter to shake some of the water off both the outside and the inside of my so-called waterproofs and to wring a significant portion of the Atlantic Ocean out of my socks. Putting them back on seemed pointless and so I resumed with naked feet inside sodden shoes. After a miserable hour and a half, during which I'd tried to detach myself mentally from my spray-filled surroundings by listing all ninety-six football league teams from north to south, I washed up early at our guest house in St David's, which was en route anyway. I'd got as far as Port Vale.

Julie hadn't yet arrived, but it wasn't difficult for the landlord to surmise that the dripping tramp at his door was one of his guests for the night and he quickly ushered Tetley and me into his garage. He was Welsh and had lived in St David's for some years.

'Where on earth have you come from?'

'From Iggly... er, Eglwyswrw today,' I revealed, 'but from Wales's northernmost point before that.'

'And are you heading for the westernmost tomorrow?' he asked – the first person I'd met, in fact, who'd latched onto the scheme of things without any convoluted explanation.

'That's right.'

'You'll be wanting directions to St David's Head then.'

'No. That's not the westernmost point.'

'Yes it is.'

'No, it isn't actually.'

'Oh yes it is. Everyone knows it is.'

I'd heard myself use this argument in other stand-offs, where eventually I'd be proven wrong: the list of false facts that 'everyone knows to be true' is long indeed. Well, so entrenched were our positions in this small dispute that we could easily have continued in this vein for several minutes, but fortunately we both grinned and agreed to consult my map. After wiping away the rain droplets, I pointed at Pen Dal-aderyn, a headland about three miles south of St David's Head and clearly half a one-kilometre grid square to the west. I didn't say anything, but neither did he. So eventually I commented:

'Of course, grid north and true north are slightly different...'

'Yes,' he agreed, 'but not that different.'

'No. So St David's Head isn't the westernmost point of the mainland, is it?'

Another pause followed, and then the landlord invoked an intriguing way of conceding defeat that left just a desperate chink of light left:

'Not on that particular map, no.'

Julie continued to prove her devotion to the support-vehicle role by cutting short the pleasures of a rainy car park in a rainy bay, to respond to the emergency mobile call and rescue me from my naked state, in a room surrounded by sodden laundry. Inevitably, as soon as I was re-clothed in non-cycling gear, the weather improved, revealing a spectacular view from our room, westward over the low, rolling fields that reach out from St David's to Ramsey Sound, which we couldn't see, and beyond to Ramsey Island, which we could.

So a walk around rain-free St David's beckoned. The place's claim to fame, outside ecclesiastical circles, is that, with a population of about 1,800, it's the smallest city in the UK. This oddity arises from the little absurdity that city status is (still) something granted by the monarch and that traditionally one reason for granting it was the presence of a cathedral – which St David's has had for some 900 years. The next smallest city, with just 7,000 residents, is the City of London.

Geographically, St David's is not a city at all but a pleasant village, albeit with only one pub – and that seemed to be closed. So for dinner we tried one of the hotels. Leave the twenty-first century behind, all ye who enter here. Whether it was intended as a time capsule or not I didn't ask, but I'd date everything about it, except the prices, to around 1965. To be fair, it was clean, neat and calm.

The unusual style started as you entered, through the sort of wire-reinforced glass door I somehow associate with a private detective's office, straight into a lounge whose tables and chairs mixed the institutional styles of an old people's home and the reading room of a theological college. The few pictures arranged haphazardly around the walls might have been left over after an unsuccessful car boot sale, while the highlights of the small bookshelf were a *Reader's Digest* guide to Spanish conquistadors and a small selection of – possibly quite valuable – children's 'annuals' from the 1950s.

While pretending to browse through a *Beezer* annual, Julie and I surveyed the other customers, half-convincing ourselves that this was indeed a theme hotel, where everyone but ourselves was in on the joke. The men and women sat at different tables. At one a lady with librarian's hair and a tasteful cardigan was explaining how many meals she could get out of a chicken. At another a bald man wearing the collar of his white cotton shirt outside his blue, crew-neck jumper was debating with his red-blazered friend the best route to Whitby.

Drinks were being carried into the lounge on round metal trays from the bar next door, but no food at all was being consumed in either. When the call came that our table was ready, we were escorted down a corridor into a separate dining room, where white linen cloths covered immaculately laid tables and where I was the only gentleman with no tie. Ordering a whole bottle of wine, we both felt a little racy – but on safer ground with the excellent roast beef and Yorkshires. The music playing softly in the background wasn't recognisable at first, but then resolved into Cliff Richard's 'The Minute You're Gone'. Spot on: 1965.

Day 16

Lunchtime with Rusty: St David's to West Point and Narberth

With another of my targets literally on the horizon – and what I was sure would be another scenic one too – I was up early and keen to get going. The westernmost point of Wales accessible without the use of a boat is Pen Dal-aderyn, opposite Ramsey Island.

The road west from St David's descended sharply to gorse-patched farmland. This area, jutting out into St George's Channel like the challenging jawline of Desperate Dan, was extensively occupied in Phases 1, 2 and 3 of the Simple History, up to Roman times. This was well before David, a Ceredigion prince, chose it as the location of his monastery in Phase 4, around the middle of the sixth century. In those days it would not have been regarded as particularly remote – quite the opposite in fact, with its easy access to important western sea routes. That morning, however, with the wind still high and the skies still ragged, it bore that craggy, threatening, edge-of-the-world feel typical of many other extremities up and down the western coasts of the British Isles.

With no luggage (to be collected on the return leg), Tetley and I sailed speedily along as far as the road would carry us, which was to a large and busy farm called Treginnis, where a surprisingly elegant woman confirmed that I was indeed permitted to take the path to the headland. Having locked Tetley and helmet to the first stile, I was oddly unencumbered as I set off smartly across the fields. With a clearing sky, views to the north were emerging. Across the first bay I could see St Justinian, home to a perilously perched lifeboat station and to the Ramsey Island ferry that runs in summer months – and when conditions permit. Beyond that the jagged line of hills that ends in St David's Head crowded the horizon.

Skirting heavy clumps of gorse on which strands of white wool had been snagged, I rambled down the gradual slope to Ramsey Sound. I'd noticed from the map that the actual westernmost spot lay opposite a group of four or five rocks that strung out from Ramsey Island and were named The Bitches. With the tidal race churning up a series of foaming rapids around them, I could see why their name might ring true for sailors – and why the odd mad kayaker has been tempted to tackle these wild waters.

Clambering over a last stile and crossing the Pembrokeshire Coast Path, which is how most people who've been here would have arrived, I was startled to see the ruins of a small stone building on the very last patch of ground before it fell away to the waves. Here I sat cross-legged to celebrate with a long swig of cold water. Seven days' cycling from the north point to this west point had felt like a lot longer. But, on reflection, it had been a tremendously varied 200 miles: dense woodland and open beaches; old railways and even older castles; comfy guest houses, intimate museums; friendly, helpful people with lots to say... and all with the constant presence of the sea nearby. I wondered whether any other 200-mile bike ride in Europe would squeeze so much in.

Sitting there, I was nearer Ireland than Swansea. In fact, a fifty-mile rail tunnel from hereabouts to the Irish mainland has been often mooted and is still not completely impossible. Out to the left, where the sound opened into St George's Channel, the next landfall was America. The nearer landfall of Ramsey Island is a bird sanctuary owned by the RSPB and I was surprised to see at the top of its cliffs, immediately above The Bitches, what looked like a substantial farm – and what I later learned to be the home of the island's two human residents.

Unlike at the windy north point, it was quite sheltered here and I could happily have stayed a while longer, but with a day's ride still ahead – and more pressingly with Julie waiting to hand over my luggage – I reluctantly left the little ruin by the sea and pointed myself at Wales's south point, over a hundred miles away in Glamorgan – and, rather sadly, my last target. First, however, I retraced my steps, and then my wheeltracks, back to St David's.

After agreeing to meet up with Julie later in Narberth, some thirty miles to the east, I set off once again, this time fully loaded. Creaking out of St David's, I noticed a house which, on closer inspection, turned out to be the most interesting in town. Evidently the home of a serious eccentric, its windows were covered in posters and notices, printed in assorted scripts and carrying various messages. One read 'Healing Hands Better than St David or British Empire'. Another cast aspersions on 'The National Trust Police'. All bore the unmistakable whiff of paranoia. Wondering if I was being filmed from behind the curtains, I smiled a rather manic smile and rode off.

Pembrokeshire is often referred to as 'Little England beyond Wales', which is a tad unfair since it's really just the southern part of the county that's been so anglicised. The Marcher lordships of Phase 5 spread across South Wales to include part of what is now southern Pembrokeshire in the twelfth century, but the north, including St David's, fell for much of the time within 'Welsh' Wales. There's even an imaginary line still dividing the two, the Landsker Line, and I must have crossed it unknowingly somewhere on my journey today.

The name Pembroke is an anglicisation of Penfro ('headland region') and Pembrokeshire today is dominated by the oil and gas industry, the terminals of which all lay to the south of my route, and by tourism. It had been noticeable to both Julie and me how much better organised for tourists this county was than our previous 'headland region', Anglesey. Pembrokeshire seemed to be covered by well-publicised bus routes, cycle routes and walking routes and the local authorities actually realised that visitors may arrive by car and may even occasionally want to park the car in order to – and here's a concept that will seem alien to Anglesey's Department of Tourism – look at the view!

Julie had given me her latest coin-ratings as follows:

- Nil-coin town: Haverfordwest
- One-coin town: Fishguard
- Two-coin towns: Cardigan and Solva (though the latter's parking is actually free)
- Three-coin town: Aberaeron

My own route for the day was town-free as I scooted due west under lightening skies, past abandoned airfields and between yellow fields of early oil seed rape, with that strong scent that annoys many but always reminds me that summer is on the way. These were quiet roads where a post van stopped to let me past as I was struggling uphill and where a young girl in a pink dressing gown waved from an upstairs room at the rare sight of a passing cyclist.

Somewhere between Hayscastle Cross and Wolf's Castle I approached a farm just as a rust-red sheepdog was being called in.

'Rusty, you naughty girl. Come off that road!'

Rusty just didn't feel inclined to obey that morning and instead lurched along the road in front of me, her occasional backward glance encouraging me to follow. Well, it was the only way to go and so I gradually caught her up. As I did so, she blocked my path, forcing a halt, and stared up at me with adoring grape-green eyes.

'Rusty,' I said sternly. 'Go home. Go home!'

In sheepdog-speak this seemed to translate as 'OK, Rusty, let's play. You lead the way.'

And so she bounded off again, but this time, with the gradient down to the valley of the Western Cleddau, I was able to overtake her and pulled up at the main A40 alone. A glance back up the hill having confirmed that Rusty had given up, I sneaked into the car park of the Wolfe Inn, quickly locked Tetley and popped inside.

The lounge was empty apart from a middle-aged couple sitting awkwardly at the bar and a barmaid who declared that the soup of the day was vegetable. Happily munching my soup-dunked roll, I couldn't help but overhear the couple's conversation:

'And so I stripped down the crank and saw the problem immediately.'

'Really?' remarked the woman. 'How clever of you.'

'Yes, it was a loose connection – which is exactly what you'd expect with the 1992 model.'

'Gosh, how fascinating. Excuse me a moment, will you, while I nip to the loo.'

If this wasn't a blind date, then I'm once again the Queen of Sheba. The crank-stripper, who evidently knew the barmaid, quickly asked her for an opinion. Her tilting hand gesture said it all and the crank-stripper looked a little disappointed, but not surprised. Tempting though it was to stay for the denouement, I collected my things and headed for the car park – where, waiting patiently beside Tetley's front wheel, was Rusty.

Either all cyclists going down that hill end up at the pub or she'd followed my scent.

'Now, Rusty,' I hissed, hands on hips, 'this is far enough. We'll walk back to the lane and you'll run off home.'

Or, in sheepdog-speak: 'Well done, Rusty. I now command you to follow me to the ends of the earth.'

So we walked, I pointed, we walked back and we sat together trying to figure out what to do. My route lay across the busy A40 and I certainly wasn't going to tempt Rusty over there. So, instructing Rusty to 'Stay here!', I went back into the bar. Rusty followed at my heel and waited outside the door.

None of the pub's staff seemed to know the name of the farmer up the hill. Directory Enquiries had no entry under the name of the farm. The blind date couple had no ideas. I was blowed if I was going to walk Rusty two miles back up the hill, just to come back down again. Eventually I rang the council's dog warden service: closed for the day. All this time I could see Rusty sitting patiently by the door, but suddenly she'd disappeared and, on going out to look for her, finally saw her mounted proudly in the passenger seat of a large tractor. Having waved the farmer down, I explained how relieved I was that he'd turned up.

'Oh, aye, she's a bugger at followin' people,' he explained, driving off, Rusty ignoring me completely. Tart!

The run from Wolf's Castle down to Narberth looked more like the classic English countryside of Sussex or Kent than West Wales. Following yesterday's rain, the sun had now come out and flowers of all shades were bursting from the hedgerows: bluebells, celandines, speedwell, ragged robin – and an odd white one that Julie identified later as alyssum. People too were bursting from their houses into the sunshine: a floppy-hatted gardener dealing with a small patch of brambles; two large, female bottoms attached to bodies that were cleaning the inside of a Ford Ka; a family of ramblers leaning over both parapets of a river bridge and apparently playing Pooh Sticks.

I wished the day's ride could go on for ever, but end it must and end it did: at the town of Narberth. Julie was waiting for me at the top of the High Street, with directions to our B&B – and with bad news about the state of it.

In terms of accommodation we'd so far had almost unbroken success, but here our luck finally ran out. Where can I start? It was a major challenge simply to get into our room, since the shape of the door-frame, which had suffered some recent catastrophe, no longer matched the shape of the door. The bed was technically a four-poster (unrequested) but, the posts being of unadorned metal and with no curtains around it, it was going to be like sleeping in a sheep pen. With a view over someone else's back door, I drew the curtains across the windows to change – thereby removing the curtain poles from the wall. Having precariously rebalanced them, I lifted the bedside light to find the switch – and watched as the lampshade's glass panels crashed to the floor. As I lifted the electric kettle, its base, attached to the dangling weight of a suspended adaptor, shot behind the wardrobe, never to be seen again.

Worst of all, however, was the bathroom. We'd already had one or two where, as Julie put it, the sealant around the shower seemed to have been applied by a Labrador's tongue. Here at the Narberth Disaster Inn, however, it looked like this had been done around 1923 and that a paintbrush had also been attached to the Labrador's tail.

We drew a small sample of these issues to the landlady's attention, who – to her credit – acknowledged them and offered us a discount.

I'd never heard of Narberth before, but it's a sizeable town for these parts , bigger than the 'city' of St David's. The High Street is a happy jumble of shops, restaurants and houses from different centuries, but somehow looking like a unified whole. At the top lies a rather steep market square, while the lower end is focused on the old town hall, an imposing, three-storey affair set in the middle of the street, with an unusual double-stairway entrance. Sited on a hillside, many of the town's streets end in a view of the nearby hills. The town developed as the centre of a Marcher lordship under the Mortimer family, and so we'd definitely dipped south of the Landsker Line here and finally left the historical 'Welsh Wales' that we'd entered eleven cycling days ago.

Narberth's not an unattractive sort of place and we managed to find a not unattractive sort of cafe, mysteriously called 'Q'. Here I chose what was trumpeted as 'Probably the best lasagne in the world' and had to concede it was certainly the best I'd tasted in Wales. What I had to leave for another time, though, was Q's 'Award-winning bara brith ice cream'

Day 17

Losing Weight and
Missing an Elephant:
Narberth to Tumble

A tough day lay ahead and the Narberth Disaster Inn's breakfast set me up well for it, recovering some kudos after the chaos of the bedroom.

It wasn't so much the scheduled distance that would make it tough (though, at over forty miles, it was a long way for me) as the fact that, for the first time since Hay, I'd be carrying my own overnight gear. For the next three days Julie would be off on business of her own and we'd meet up again at our final overnight stop, in Cardiff. I'd pared down my load to the bare minimum and therefore now offer Guise's Six Top Tips for Lightweight Cycle Touring:

- Choose your worst socks and pants so that you can throw them away each night.
- Plan to wear the next day's cycling gear the evening before. After all, you probably won't be eating at The Ritz.
- You'll be too knackered to read and so won't need any books.
- Don't treat your bike as a mobile sweet shop; buy supplies en route instead.
- Have your hair cut and nails trimmed. Men: think ears, nose and chin too.
- After each snack at premises with facilities, answer the call of nature before setting off again.

So, it was with a relaxed constitution and a streamlined face that I waved goodbye to my number-one supporter and headed for the coast. The countryside continued to feel very English, but more overnight rain and an overcast start had dulled the colours and seemingly calmed down the local bird life, which kept unnaturally quiet until I passed Silence Farm, where not only chickens but dogs belied the intriguing name of their home.

In fact, having escaped the Aber- and Llan-obsessed west of Wales, I now began to pass several more candidates for *The Meaning of Liff*: crinow (noun) – crease in a sock that occurs only when enclosed in a shoe and only next to the most sensitive part of the foot; tavernspite (noun) – unfocussed desire for confrontation that overcomes certain people (mostly men) after the fourth pint.

I'd also entered Carmarthenshire, one of the original Phase 5 (thirteenth century) counties of Wales, but one which was rashly swallowed by Dyfed in 1974, only to be spat out again in 1996. The corner of the county I traversed this morning was the undulating landscape of a low plateau, until I dived down to the coast at Pendine (pronounced '-dine', not '-dean'). The suddenness and bendiness of the descent quickly had me off the bike and walking – in fact walking next to an intriguing escape lane signposted for cars but wide enough only for two-wheeled vehicles.

Stretching out to the east from Pendine village is a seven-mile beach whose flat and firm surface led, for a period, to its fame. By 1924, when Ernest Eldridge raised the world land speed record to 146 mph, the wisdom of allowing such activity on public roads was unsurprisingly being questioned. Eldridge's record had been set on a French road, but even performing such feats at the Brooklands circuit in Surrey was considered too dangerous and so it was to Pendine Sands that Malcolm Campbell and Welshman John Parry-Thomas turned, raising the bar right here, over three years and five records, to 174 mph. In 1927, however, Parry-Thomas was killed during his latest attempt, becoming – with unwanted notoriety reminiscent of Charles Rolls's seventeen years before – the first Briton killed attempting a world speed record. Thereafter, Campbell moved his operations to Daytona Beach, Florida.

This morning the fastest thing on Pendine Sands was the retreat from the chilly waters of Carmarthen Bay by about thirty squealing, yellow-helmeted, teenage body-surfers. The speed connection was still present, though, in the form of the Museum of Speed. At least, it was there on the map – oh, not another Cheese Centre, surely – no, I just passed a sign to it. Where could it be? Scanning around the jumble of beachside buildings, I noticed one bearing no sign: a low, modern black affair, which I approached along a path consisting of small bumps evidently designed to discourage any approach. And yet, on opening the door, this was clearly it. The reluctance to advertise itself had worked: for the third Welsh museum in a row, I was the only customer.

It was rather small and unfortunately today did not include Babs, Parry-Thomas's record-breaking vehicle, which is exhibited here from time to time. What was here though was well-documented and, to me, very informative. I hadn't known that in 1933 Amy Johnson and her husband took off from here to cross the Atlantic, the runway at Croydon having proven too short for her fuel-laden aircraft. Nor that, prior to Campbell and crew's arrival, Pendine Sands was already an established race track – as shown by the photos on display, in which unprotected spectators watched racing cars speed by at horrifyingly close quarters. Since World War Two, the sands have been owned by the Ministry of Defence, which still uses it as a firing range: hence the numerous warnings about unexploded bombs.

Taking the relatively safe A4066, and adopting my standard, sedate 5 mph, I trundled off towards Laugharne.

If Dylan Thomas had been smart, he would have toured his favourite hotels and bars throughout Wales at no cost at all other than a signed note proclaiming that he'd done something there: written a few lines, drunk a few beers, stroked the dog, winked at the barmaid... whatever. The number of Thomas-related tourist signs scattered about Wales suggests that there's serious money to be made from any connection at all. Laugharne's connection, though, is rock solid: your man lived here for four years, down at the Boathouse, now a museum. Its location, along with that of Laugharne Castle and of the village in general, is certainly picturesque: Laugharne hovers on low shelves just above the lower tidal reaches of the River Taf, as it winds its way to join two other estuaries before squeezing past the vast sands to empty into Carmarthen Bay.

Going north out of Laugharne, the road rises sharply and I stopped now and then to try, without success, to get a glimpse across the valley of Trefenty Farm. Here, almost 400 years before, William Lower set up one of Britain's earliest telescopes and became one of the first to observe closely the Moon's craters and Halley's Comet.

As if they knew I was thinking about them, the heavens suddenly opened and I was lucky this time to be passing a pub in St Clears. A light lunch called and I duly responded, adding a burst of coffee and a quick transformation in the gents into my wet-weather personality. Suitably equipped, I emerged and remounted – just as the rain eased up.

There was no point in changing back again now, and so I followed the NCN 4 signs – or as many of them as I could see without my specs (useless in the rain) – but succeeded only in joining the traffic on the A40 dual carriageway, as it thundered its way towards the Hanger Lane Gyratory System, over 200 miles and a world away in London. Through some kind of insanity, I pedalled along this hard shoulder, within a few centimetres of twelve-metre petrol tankers and continental coaches, for a good three miles before eventually peeling off into the comparative silence of Bancyfelin village. From here I clambered up a few drippy glades and down a few scrunchy lanes until I'd rejoined NCN 4.

Have you heard about the masochist who liked to take a cold shower at six o'clock every morning? So he didn't. What he did do, I suspect, is get a job in the routing department at Sustrans, since only a masochist could think that the steep, winding route through Llangynog is the best way to cycle into Carmarthen. The sharp east wind didn't help either and by the time I creaked into the county town to have a glug of water at the foot of a giant monument to Sir Thomas Picton (a Pembrokeshire soldier who died at the Battle of Waterloo), I was some way behind schedule.

However, I was keen to find an elephant and therefore turned off the main road. I'm not suggesting that elephants are often found grazing here, just that my research had indicated that, some time ago, such a beast was in the employ of a travelling circus when it was taken ill in this very town, died and was buried under a field next to Richmond Terrace. Finding my way through Carmarthen's back streets, I tried to pin down what it was that made this place look unmistakably Welsh. The streets were nicely wiggly, but then so are many all over

Britain. The pavements were narrow or absent, but so are Cornwall's. The small buildings weren't unusual either… and then it was suddenly obvious. Not only were the shops, houses, pubs and offices all small-scale, but they were also all unpretentious. Not unattractive, but not – as is so often the case elsewhere in Britain – vying for notoriety, with a classical column here and a shiny brass knocker there. Unlike Aberaeron, which I now recognised as looking not just odd, but oddly un-Welsh, Carmarthen seemed quite content with itself as it was, and as it had always been.

These suburban reflections brought me to Richmond Terrace, which had a field of sorts on both sides. Next to the field in front of the county offices, I pulled up beside a lady pushing a buggy.

'Excuse me, do you know if there's an elephant buried under this field?'

'Er, no, no – I didn't see anything.' And with that she hurried on her way.

With no one else around, I tried my luck at the sports ground opposite, where an elderly gentleman was walking unsteadily away from town.

'Excuse me, do you know if there's an elephant buried under this field?'

'Eh? Hey, no I don't, boy – but if you whistle it, I'll try to sing along. Ha!'

Though I laughed at the old joke I couldn't dissuade him from staggering off, giggling to himself, and so gave up.

At the lowest bridging point on the River Towy, Carmarthen is possibly the oldest town in Wales. It was recorded by

Ptolemy, formed the local Roman *civitas* and seems to have thrived through all phases of Welsh history. Pedalling through the narrow streets of the medieval walled town, and past the statue of Sir William Nott, an eighteenth-century Carmarthen innkeeper who became a general in the British army in India, I noticed that some areas had become rather tatty. However, it was certainly still thronged – and occasionally clogged up – with traffic. Roads seem to shoot off in all directions and, spectacles now reinstated, I followed the signs carefully until safely on the B4300, which forms part of NCN 47 and runs close to the picturesque south bank of the Towy – too close at one point, where recent river erosion had undercut the roadway and forced it to a single track.

My next target involved one of the more bizarre references in the *Encyclopaedia*. In 2002 the village of Llanddarog was, it declares, voted the friendliest place in Wales. By whom? Llanddarog residents? The millions of visitors who come here rather than to Cardiff? It doesn't say. Nor have I been able to discover the answer. I had, however, expected to be able to test the claim myself – but alas, in late afternoon, Llanddarog was completely deserted... except for a young woman who took one look at me before dashing into the parish church – presumably to offer a friendly prayer for my salvation.

As I left Llanddarog, I was leaving one version of Wales and entering another. It was a change I'd been expecting – and somewhere on the road from Llanddarog to Tumble it occurred: rural Wales ended and industrial Wales began. Where communities had huddled around the church, chapel and pub, they now strung themselves along the roads. Where ancient cottages had happily rubbed shoulders with modern developments, nineteenth-century terraces now hunched their shoulders against the world. Where timeless fields and woods had spread behind the villages, now the leftovers of a recent industrial past were scattered across the landscape.

On the edge of Tumble, a new woodland park called Mynydd Mawr ('great mountain') had emerged on the site of the Great Mountain Colliery, an anthracite pit opened in 1887 and closed in 1962. The village of Tumble itself, which was my destination for the night, had mostly been built to house colliery workers and, in pushing Tetley up its steep and bleak main street, I passed the Great Mountain Working Men's Club, two or three dodgy-looking takeaways and an almost unbroken line of cars, many in an advanced state of disrepair, parked in front of the terraced homes. A difference from the rural villages that I hadn't been expecting was the eagerness to greet me among people in the street.

'Right?' shouted a young man cleaning his Vauxhall Nova.

'Right?' called a cyclist whizzing in the opposite direction.

'Right?' mumbled a boy eating his chips outside one of the takeaways.

In fact, this one-word greeting, which I imagine is short for 'Are you all right?' accompanied me right across South Wales and I always responded likewise – at least when my breath would allow me. It's possible of course that everyone was genuinely concerned about my state of health.

Anyway, I eventually panted through a gateway on which the name of my accommodation was painted and followed a long, cinder track past a large barn, two large goats and three large guinea fowl to a large door. A large woman answered. This being my first ever farmhouse B&B, I was a little unsure of the drill, but the farmer's wife sat me at the kitchen table and explained who everyone was, including the various dogs sniffing around, and how everything worked. All very interesting, but my priority was food – and, since no mention was made of there being any for me here and since I was half a mile down a track in the middle of nowhere, it seemed that even at this late hour another bike ride was on the cards – on a bicycle with no lights.

Having dumped my big blue bag it was therefore with some urgency that I scrunched off up the track again to Cross Hands, two miles to the north and, I hoped, more blessed with sit-down food than Tumble.

Arriving in Cross Hands was like riding into *Dead Man's Gulch*. The place was deserted, save for a few dogs on the sidewalk, tumbleweed blowing down Main Street and a pack of mean-looking critters rolling out of a downtown bar. The critters were all female, all wore cowgirl hats and most wore cowgirl boots too. As they piled into a minibus, I pulled up outside the pub from which they'd just been ejected – the only one in town it seemed – locked up Tetley and went inside. Plenty of spare tables, but alas no food tonight.

Across the street was a Tandoori restaurant: plenty of food, but alas no tables for an hour. It had been only a few hours since I'd left my support team and it looked to me like I might soon starve to death. To the rescue, however, came the lights of a chip shop: 'Eat Here Or Take Away'. I did both. My 'take away' course was consumed in front of an estate agent's window. House prices so far on this trip had been pretty high – most a little higher than equivalent properties in the Midlands, some much higher – but here in Cross Hands and Tumble they took a... well, a tumble. For the price of a one-bed flat in the Midlands you could snap up a semi here. It didn't look as though this estate agent had been selling many of late, though, as at least half the cards were curled up and falling off the rack.

Dusk was falling by the time my weary little legs got me back to the farm and pretty soon, they were showered, towelled and horizontal little legs, out for the count.

Day 18

The Great Storm of Swansea Bay: Tumble to Briton Ferry

While his wife ruled indoors, the farmer ruled outdoors and I came across him before breakfast as I retrieved my bike from one of his barns. A solid-looking, grey-haired chap in wellies, dirty jeans and a woolly jumper padded at elbow and shoulder, he seemed pleased to have someone to talk to. In a broad accent from the West Country (of England), he explained how moving from Dorset to this fourteen-acre smallholding was the best move they'd ever made. As well as the animals I'd seen, they had several horses and rode them wherever they could. The land was mostly put to grass and most of his work to date had been in erecting the outbuildings that stood around us.

'You mean you built them yourself?' I asked.

'With my own 'ands, aye.'

'How did you design them?'

'Design? Well, I does it as I goes along, I s'pose. Mind, I'd got a good start with these supports.'

'They look like telegraph poles.'

'That's 'cause they are telegraph poles,' he laughed. '1940s, I think. I got a friend who works for BT an' they was goin' to throw 'em away. What a waste! Got about fifty of 'em. 'E drove 'em in for me an' all.'

Telling him about my search for food in Cross Hands the previous evening, I asked if I'd missed any restaurant there.

'Oh, Cross 'Ands. Dunno. Ain't been there for months. Don't leave my own little empire if I can 'elp it.'

Re-entering his wife's empire, I ate two six-minute eggs while she chatted away in the kitchen, filling me in on the ups and downs of running a rural B&B. I asked why she thought so many of the couples 'escaping to the country' on TV made such a mess of setting up a similar business.

'Oh, it's a twenty-four-hour-a-day job,' she explained. 'You've got to accept that up front. Most of them don't and so they fail. Simple.'

Fair comment. Wishing them both well, I made a brave show of pedalling a fully loaded Tetley up the track – until I was out of sight and immediately out of the saddle, pushing the rest of the way to the main road.

The weather was grey and cool, but if it stayed that way I'd be lucky, as the forecast was dire, to say the least. Foul weather was due in from the east and already the wind that had blown the weeds around in Cross Hands had strengthened, turning its attentions to buckets and bins. Before I turned off a mile down the road I'd already rescued two dustbins and a road sign from the middle of the street.

So an off-road section was particularly welcome and at the entrance to the Celtic Trail (aka NCN 47) a large sign first listed all the authorities responsible for putting it at my disposal, before advising me that it also helped the Welsh Assembly Government meet European Union Objective One. I'm sure you're as eager as I was to know what this is. The reference is, I believe, Objective One of the EU's 'Structural Funds', which aims to 'support development in the less prosperous regions'. Well, someone had evidently decided that Tumble tumbles into this category and I, for one, was delighted they had, since it gave me the rare opportunity of benefiting from my own taxes by breezing down the most splendid cycle track I've ever had the pleasure of riding on.

At once I was transported from the grey back streets of Tumble into a dense green jungle of trees, bushes, valleys and streams, through all of which the cycle route swept with the most delectably gradual downhill gradient, as though oblivious to the terrain around it. What it most resembled was a breathtaking canopy walk through a Costa Rican rainforest, but what it actually comprised was, not surprisingly, another old railway trackbed – very old in this case, for the long-disused Llanelly and Mynydd

Mawr Railway had itself inherited the route from the Carmarthenshire Tramroad, a private, horse-drawn line established in 1802 to carry coal from Tumble to the ironworks and docks in Llanelli.

For ten glorious miles it carried me along this same route, not only giving my old legs a well-deserved break but also protecting the rest of me from the gathering wind, which I could hear whipping at the treetops, but which, cocooned in my green tunnel, I could barely feel at all.

Among the miscellaneous overlapping names of the Sustrans cycle network in Wales, the Celtic Trail is in fact 377 miles of interweaving routes all across South Wales between Fishguard and Chepstow. This short stretch from Tumble to Llanelli, which I strongly recommend, is also known as the Swiss Valley Cycleway. As I approached Llanelli, the landscape to the east could indeed be perceived – in a bad light, through squinted eyes and with a lot of imagination – as being vaguely alpine.

After a long, lovely but lonesome trail, the Ninth Law of Cycle Touring told me I was once again approaching civilisation:

When you hit the dog-walkers, you're about to hit town.

The part of town I hit was Felinfoel, a name familiar to many from the brewery named after it, which lay just beyond the trees to the left. Following rapidly on its heels, but again out of sight beyond the trees, was another beer connection: Parc Howard mansion, built in 1885 by the

Buckley family, whose own brewery had been founded by the Reverend James Buckley, after whom was named The Rev. James bitter that I'd tasted on my very first night in Monmouth.

Where there's beer there's often rugby and indeed, standing proudly to the right of the cycle track was Stradey Park, home of Llanelli RFC, known nowadays as Llanelli Scarlets. Now, I know a thing or two about rugby. Two in fact: you can't pass forwards and you can't kick backwards. Or is it the other way round? All right, I admit I'm an ignorant *Saeson*, but I did know that the traditional Welsh rugby anthem *'Sospan Fach'* ('Little Saucepan') is based on the tin saucepans that supposedly adorned the top of the posts at Stradey Park, in honour of Llanelli's long association with the tin industry. I just had to check this out and so wheeled Tetley across the empty car park and up to the stadium's gates. There, on posts at the top of the scoreboard, they were: two tiny, red saucepans. With their lids sealed on of course: you don't want any pigeon incidents, do you? (Five months after I passed by, and 129 years after it opened, the last game was played at Stradey Park. The stadium was demolished, the team moved to a new multi-million-pound stadium and the old saucepans were auctioned off – just in time for a new set to be made, by local firm Dyfed Steels, for the top of the new stadium's posts.)

Beer? Saucepans? I was getting slightly peckish but, due to an unfortunate misunderstanding with the signposts, Tetley and I ended up climbing through a gap in a fence onto the ring road and missing the North Dock cafe – a mistake with more significance than I realised at the time.

The fortunes of Llanelli ('the sacred place of St Elli') were so tied up with the development of the thirty-one tinplate mills that the town boasted in the nineteenth century that it was also known as Tinopolis. Located on the Loughor estuary, it used to have five docks too, the last of which closed in 1952, and it's the old dock area that has since become the Millennium Coastal Park, a remarkable area of grasslands and wetlands that should be a model for how to make the best of a derelict industrial site.

Making the best of the still dry weather, I struggled against the brisk easterly for four miles around the headland, admiring the views over the tidal flats to the Gower where, on the right day, you might just imagine you're on the edge of the Mediterranean. In front of a huddle of modern flats a group of hardy yuccas flapped in the wind.

It was quite a relief to leave Tetley locked up outside the National Wetland Centre as I headed inside for a snack – and quite a disappointment to head straight back out again, having clocked the £6 charge for entering.

There followed two more miles around another windy headland, this time admiring the strange, grey bulk of the Trostre Tinplate Works, looking like The Devil's Lego Set. The sights even of Llanelli began to pale after a while, though, and as I hit the main road I was keen to move on – though not before reflecting on the famous names that had been born or brought up here: rugby players Phil Bennett and Jonathan Davies; world snooker champion Terry Griffiths, BBC newsreader Huw Edwards, Donald Swann (the pianist half of 1960s duo Flanders and Swann) and Brian Trubshaw, Concorde test pilot and one-time hero for young boys. As eclectic a list as you'd find anywhere.

So many well-known names reminded me that I had now definitely entered that part of Wales where the bulk of its people live. Llanelli had 45,000 residents, but no reasonable coffee to offer me on my admittedly rather unusual route through their town. Next stop, across the bridge over the Loughor, was Gorseinon, home to nearly 8,000 and birthplace of former Conservative leader Michael Howard (whose Romanian family had taken their British surname from Llanelli's Parc Howard)... but also home to just one shop that was closed and one pub not yet open. The NCN signs took me on a futile route behind some houses and straight into a concrete wall, before eventually finding a way under the railway tracks and into the village of Gowerton. No shops or cafes of course but, taking a break in a bus shelter I did find in the depths of my kit half a Milky Bar that I'd forgotten about and snaffled it like a cat who'd come across an unexpected fish.

Just as I'd finished, heavy raindrops began to patter on the roof of the shelter and so I took the opportunity to don my so-called waterproofs. It proved to be my last good move of the day.

Following another leafy old railway route, NCN 4 (into which NCN 47 had morphed without telling me) gently lowered me towards Swansea Bay. A mile or so from the coast the lights of a pub shone through the trees and then glittered in the puddles as I passed the entrance, right next to the track. Even now I'm not certain why I pedalled by, but I believe I might have fancied a cafe with a sea view.

Emerging at Black Pill, between The Mumbles and Swansea, I splashed across the main road and up onto the promenade. The view that greeted me there couldn't have been wilder if I'd just scrambled over the brow at Cape Horn and gazed over the Antarctic Ocean. The whole of the earth and the sea seemed to be alive: bushes, trees and flagpoles swayed hysterically; sand flew savage, brown clouds across the vast beach towards The Mumbles, two miles to the south; and on the sea itself, complete mayhem reigned. Evil grey waves churned up a ragged, rocking surf that hurled a thousand fistfuls of spray up at the low, broken edges of the glowering clouds.

It was at the same time magnificent and mesmerising. It was only when a lone jogger, perhaps as dazed as I, blew past on a gust of wind that I realised my left side was already drenched, while my right would have immediately become so had I simply turned around. Scuttling into the semi-sanctuary offered by the leeward side of a hoarding, I checked that all the pockets of my bag were safely sealed and considered what to do. No cafe nor even shelter was in sight. The sensible thing to have done would be retreat to the trees and retrace my steps to the pub, there to sit out the storm in the dry warmth of a lounge bar. The actual thing I did, for reasons unknown, was to leap back into the saddle, push off into the teeth of the storm and head for Swansea, shouting 'Chaaaarge!'

Westerlies must blow nine days out of ten here, but today, on my north-easterly route along the edge of Swansea Bay, the wind blew directly into my face. The precipitation, which had already been torrential, now became horizontal too, but whether it was rain or hail or sand or road grit that peppered my face and hands I didn't know. What I did know was that, with my mouth fixed open through the effort of pedalling – in the lowest gear and on the flat – it peppered my tongue too. An interesting experience. From time to time, a gust blew Tetley sideways and I had to dismount or else crash down to the beach – but even walking is a challenge when the wind lifts your feet off the ground for you. Needless to say, I was soaked completely to the skin – and probably beyond.

Parallel to Swansea's promenade runs a dual carriageway, preventing any cycle access to the town, and, from the vehicles halted at traffic lights, faces peered with pity, sympathy and sometimes horror at the deranged cyclist progressing at a zigzag 0.5 mph through the worst storm of the year. No one else was on the path. No one else was even outside their vehicles.

After an unknown length of time (my watch having been consigned to the deepest recess of my blue bag), a choice presented itself ahead of me: follow the cycle track on its insane shore-side trajectory or take a road through some half-finished apartment blocks. Choosing the apartments, I stepped carefully around the fences, tubs and small items of machinery that had been blown into the road and eventually found myself by a large marina, whose vessels rocked angrily in the wind, but where the gale had actually eased enough for me to raise my head and take stock. Over there was Swansea city centre, which must surely mean food. How to get from over here to over there? Still no one was around and so I wandered about until a footbridge appeared and then a car park and then an alley and finally a street with people and restaurants. It was called Wind Street.

As I trundled Tetley beside wine bars, steak houses and pizzerias, staring at dry people eating warm food, I gradually accepted the sad truth: I was a wreck. It may not actually be illegal to sit in Lloyds No.1 Bar dripping a large part of the Atlantic Ocean on the floor, but even a half-drowned rat has standards. Reluctantly I pointed my rumbling stomach west again.

Although I'd optimistically filled my notebook in advance with the sights I might sample in Swansea, to me on that day, Wales's second city was just one big storm. The *Encyclopaedia* reveals that Swansea is Britain's wettest city. Tell me about it.

The wind having eased a little and the rain having actually stopped at last, progress along the cycle track beside the A483 dual carriageway was steady and I was soon able to pull in at a petrol station where I thought my dilapidated state might not result in immediate ejection. There I gathered a handful of goodies – for the record, a Yorkie Bar, a Boost, a cheese and pickle sandwich and a Tango – and consumed them with a storm-ravaged stare, sitting on the kerb next to the air pump.

The only thing on my mind was Briton Ferry – and it's not often that anyone has said that. This former port on the River Neath, an outlet for the bigger town of Neath itself, was where I'd booked in for the night, and after another long stint by the A483 and a weary haul across the bridge, high above the river, I finally knocked on the door of my B&B.

I was early. Having lost track of time somewhere in the chaos of Swansea Bay, I now realised that I'd actually had all the time I wanted to find somewhere dry to sit out the storm. Even though the weather seemed to have knocked any common sense out of me, I had nevertheless battled through to my destination and was looking forward to the evening of recovery I felt I deserved. So it was some relief that, although she wasn't really open yet, my landlady sized up the situation pretty fast and let me in. Having peeled off my sodden garments, one disastrous layer after another, and verified that my feet, which had developed the colour and texture of marshmallows, would not need amputating after all, I took a long, lazy shower and an even longer, lazier nap.

Unlike Tumble or Cross Hands, Briton Ferry has an ordinary pub that does ordinary food and it's here that I presented myself early that evening, looking almost human again. Just as the barmaid was taking my food order, however, a scuffle could be heard outside, followed by a loud groan and the hasty entrance of a short, stocky man – presumably the assailant – who marched over to a table occupied by a young lady and two children and sat down beside them. Ten seconds later the door burst open again as a taller man, wearing a 'Wales RFU' shirt, dishevelled hair and with his left eye in a visibly poor state, staggered in, followed immediately by a second, who enveloped the first in a restrictive bear hug.

What followed left a considerable impression on me. First, the young lady had a severe word in the stocky man's ear, concerning behaviour in front of children, took them with her and left. Next, the barmaid, a woman short of stature but solid of build, marched to within an inch of the victim and his bear, looked up at both and gave them ten seconds to leave the premises. They did so. Carefully ignoring the assailant, she then made a short phone call before returning to the bar, picking up her pencil and pad and saying to me:

'… and after the pâté?'

Shortly after I'd sat down, a tall man with an air of authority entered, looked over at the stocky assailant, who had been sitting quietly with his pint, jerked his thumb to an empty table in the corner and watched him walk over to it. There followed a quiet nose-to-nose conversation between the two, during which most of the colour drained from the assailant's face and at the end of which he left, his pint unfinished. Reporting to the barmaid, the tall man said just one word:

'Sorted.'

I don't expect they had any more trouble for a while.

Day 19

Not the End of It: Briton Ferry to Cardiff

This was to be my last full day and I was away at eight o'clock sharp. I knew I should really have gone north to take in the Miners' Museum in the Vale of Neath, but I had a pretty good idea of what that would involve. What a Stones Museum would be, however, I couldn't guess at all – surely the interest to be gleaned from a few stones would be limited to a small trayful at most. Intrigued, I headed south towards Margam.

Joining the coastal cycle route again, I was directed for a noisy mile alongside the A48 dual carriageway where, astonishingly, a row of new houses had been inserted on a narrow site between the traffic and a vertical cliff face. Hoping they were triple-glazed and that their occupants were out at work all day, I turned off into the relative peace of Baglan Bay.

This is the first of two 'communities' I was due to pass through today whose resident population, according to the *Encyclopaedia*, was exactly zero. In the case of Baglan Bay, this is because it is entirely occupied by an oil refinery, a chemical works and the oddly named Baglan Energy Park. The entrance to the latter was marked by a proud and sturdy rock bearing its name, next to which flapped a flimsy hardboard sign announcing something easier to understand: 'Aunty Ann's Cafe'.

Resisting the temptation to stock up only an hour after breakfast, I pedalled on and emerged in front of the broad, flat expanse of Aberavon Sands. This was not what I'd been expecting. Stretching from Port Talbot, a mile to the east, and as far as the eye could see to the west was the most pristine beach I'd ever seen – and that includes Pendine, as well as many around the Mediterranean and on the Pacific and Indian Oceans. What made the sight even more remarkable was that this was still part of Swansea Bay, scene of yesterday's mayhem and which arced round as far as Mumbles Head under a heavy and still threatening sky. The two factors responsible for the billiard-table smoothness of the beach were the outgoing tide and a single blue tractor, pulling behind it a lime-green beach-smoother (possibly not its technical name) along a series of parallel lines that would take its driver the best part of the day to complete.

Dragging my eyes away from the mesmerising beach scene, I scanned up and down the promenade to discover that this too was completely litter-free. Somewhere at the far western end of Swansea Bay there must have been a pile of wind-blown litter the size of a castle after the stormy day before. Sixty years ago the land between here and the main road formed a vast area of sand dunes, but in the 1950s they were replaced by the Sandfields housing estate, built to house workers from the steelworks to the south-east, whose towers and port installations dominated the eastern horizon.

It's towards them that I cycled, exchanging a quick comment on the weather with the odd jogger and dog-walker. Offering no comment at all – nor any explanation for their location on the grass by the promenade – were a series of low and rather weathered concrete penguins perched on a series of even lower concrete icebergs. Rounding the corner by the long arms of the deep-water tidal docks, opened in 1972 to handle the iron ore that feeds the steelworks, I passed the mandatory twenty-first-century sea-front apartments, with their mandatory yuccas, but this time less dominant than Swansea's rather pretentious multi-storey blocks. Then came another surprise: a row of colourful little fishing boats, tied up against the grassy banks of the River Afon (the Afon Afon, as it were), a reminder of the days before industrial development transformed this whole coastline.

I assumed that the dilapidated town centre I crossed was Port Talbot's, although there was nothing to confirm this. Passing the Gas Welfare Club, the Wing Wai Fish Bar and the abandoned 'Vivia_ Pa_k Ho_el' (which I imagine used to have a few more letters), I briefly rejoined the A48, where a German lorry driver sat asleep in his cab in a lay-by, before NCN 4 guided me into the back streets and another quiet housing estate.

This was Margam and the 'community' beyond the railway was Margam Moors, the other one with no residents at all, for it is now entirely a steelworks, known colloquially as the 'Abbey Works', whose blast furnaces, chimneys and other mammoth structures overwhelm about three miles of coastline. Originally built by the Steel Company of Wales in 1952, its then workforce of 18,000 made it the biggest employer in Wales and the biggest steelworks in Europe. Since then, its ownership has reflected the history of steelmaking in Britain in general: nationalised under Wilson as part of the British Steel Corporation in 1967; privatised under Thatcher in 1988; merged with a Dutch group to form Corus in 1999; and taken over by India's Tata Steel in 2007. It now produces five million tonnes of steel slab a year. Personally, I don't know what a million tonnes of steel would look like, but it's a fair guess that it's a lot.

On the other side of the tracks, beyond the dual carriageway and the motorway, behind a little rusty gate and squeezed up against the steep wooded slopes of Margam Mountain lies tiny Margam village itself, and it's here that I dismounted in front of the Stones Museum. It was closed, but a notice told me I could collect the keys from a nearby cafe. (Perhaps all Welsh museums expect only one visitor at a time.) The cafe was closed too.

However, the thoughtful managers of this particular museum had filled the front wall of the small barn that housed it with sheet glass and through this I could see quite clearly what type of stones it comprised: not the type that you find on a beach, but the type that you find sticking out of a hillside or graveyard. Ah, I see: *standing* stones.

An information board, which I could read if I screwed my neck around, explained that the stones gathered here, of which there appeared to be only about a dozen, covered a period of 1,300 years and that some had originated from the various religious establishments that used to occupy what is now Margam Country Park. And that one of them contained an inscription written in Irish Ogam (I think I could spot the one), which would make it very rare indeed.

Noting that time was getting on and that the route to Cardiff looked pretty arduous, I forsook the contour-laden route proposed by Sustrans and trundled instead along the main road for a while before rejoining the cycle route about three miles further on. After some help...

As I was walking Tetley along a street of modest houses in Kenfig Hill, a pink Ford Fiesta with tinted windows pulled over, its driver's window wound down and, to my surprise, an elderly gentleman with grey hair and a genial face leaned over.

'Sorry,' I said. 'I probably can't direct you. I'm not from round here.'

'No, but I am,' he replied in a local accent, 'and I can probably direct you.'

'To where?'

'To the cycle track you're looking for: you've just passed it.'

Turning round, I saw he was right and thanked him, but he called me back.

'Where you headed?' he asked.

'Er, Cardiff today.'

'Oh, a long-distance job! Good for you. Where've you come from?'

I told him.

'Oh, even better,' he said, grinning… and then added the standard: 'Fair play to you, boy.' He leaned a little closer. 'You know, twelve years ago, when I was sixty-three, I walked all around the coast of Wales.'

'Fair play to *you*,' I put in.

'In stages of course. But listen, son, (and here he waggled his index finger) that's not the end of it! Do you read the *Western Mail*?'

I admitted I didn't.

'Well, I used to buy it, but now I reads it down the library for free, but anyway, a few weeks ago there was an article about a man who'd walked all the way round Britain! Can you believe that?'

'It certainly sounds impressive.'

'It does indeed. But… (more finger waggling) that's not the end of it! This man was eighty-four!'

'Blimey.'

'Blimey indeed. Well, I *buys* a copy of that edition, don't I, and takes it home… and that's not the end of it either! I telephones this eighty-four-year-old man and congratulates him!'

'Fair enough. And did it inspire you to put on your walking boots again?'

'Oh, legs aren't what they used to be, son. Drive everywhere now. Oh, by the way, this isn't my car, it's my granddaughter's. Mine's down the garage. Look pretty stupid, don't I?'

Before I could think of a response, he'd wound up the window and may well have waved me on my way – but all I could see in the tinted glass was my own helmeted reflection.

NCN 4 now set off along another disused railway track, lined with willow and oak, rowan and hawthorn – and another idyllic stretch for long-distance cyclists. Idyllic, that is, apart from the three spots where large branches had fallen across it in yesterday's storms, all of which were just passable – though in one case, only by sliding Tetley on its side and crawling along on my stomach behind it. In fact, everything from twiglets to whole trees was strewn along the next four miles of track as far as the old mining village of Tondu, now an outer suburb of Bridgend.

The route had held to the high ground for a while now, and just before it dipped to the lowland, where three rivers meet to form the Ogmore Valley, a rather touching monument stood a little way back from the cycle track. In 1892 an underground explosion in the Park Slip Colliery killed 112 men and boys and the monument to their memory comprises 112 large stones neatly packed together to form a giant cone.

In Tondu itself, the sun came out just as a small grocer's and newsagent's appeared around the corner and, recalling my two recent brushes with starvation, this time I didn't let the opportunity pass, as I sat on the step, munching a scrumptious turkey and cranberry roll and reading in amazement about a cricket match that England had actually won. All was not well with my fellow earthlings, however, as one souped-up car after another pulled in outside a nearby chip shop and disgorged their male, baseball-capped occupants, who shouted back to their girlfriends, still being deafened by the high-volume bass in the cars, such endearments as:

'F***! Thirrouta Coke!'

and,

'Oy, Shaz, d'ya wanna pastie with tha' or wa'?!'

Apart from the shouting, Tondu didn't seem too bad a place, but I was glad nevertheless to resume along another glade-like, traffic-free track beside the River Ogmore as far as Blackmill. From here things slowed down considerably, as Sustrans's resident masochist – or, if they don't cycle themselves, which seemed possible, their resident sadist – took over the routing again. NCN 4 commenced a four-mile run along the A4093, almost all of which I was obliged to walk. If the only route available is too steep for cycling, then this means it is not, by definition, a cycle route – and sticking little blue-and-red signs onto the lampposts will never make it one.

The views were nice, though. If the coal and iron industries hadn't transformed the Valleys in the nineteenth century, then they would be a spectacular continuation of rural Mid-Wales. Even some of the old mining towns now have a kind of grandeur, given their location and the disappearance of almost all their industry, and Gilfach Goch is a classic example. Sitting astride the steep valley of Ogwr Fach it clings to the green slopes below Maesteg Mountain and offers a defiant grey stare southwards to the rest of the world. Its position is not unlike that of a typical Alpine ski resort and I couldn't help wondering how it would look if an Aberaeron-type colour scheme were tried on the terraced houses.

Pedalling through Tonyrefail (the place that sounds more like a chain of convenience stores than a Welsh village), I had only one more upland haul to make before Pontypridd, from where the map promised me a long, downhill swoop to Cardiff. Just out of Tonyrefail, my eye was caught by an old, worn plaque on the gatepost of a farm and I pulled over to read it. It had been placed there almost a hundred years before and recorded an event nearly 600 years before that. It read:

Pant-y-Brâd
Opposite on
Nov 16th 1326 was captured
King Edward 2nd
(Edward of Caernarvon)
The guide of captors was
Rev. Rhys Hywel (Rhys o'r Mynydd)

It's no surprise that a 'Rev.' had a hand in the king's capture, since the church took a dim view of Edward II's alleged homosexuality. Whether Rev. Rhys Hywel anticipated the gruesome death that would befall Edward the following year is unknown.

Struggling over one more brow of one more hill, I was at last relieved to see a broad view to the south-east open out, including, to the right, Llantwit Fardre – 'the steward's house of the sacred place of Illtud', not of Twit, which is a rather cruel anglicisation. To the left, the roofs and towers of Pontypridd sat neatly in the deep, urbanised valley of the River Taff. Still pretending that these steep, narrow roads constituted a cycle route, NCN 4 dropped me sharply down through the suburbs and then suddenly into the middle of the rush-hour traffic of downtown Pontypridd, next to a spectacularly ugly tower called 'Sardis House'.

Here Sustrans's little signs completely disappeared. I was looking for NCN 8, aka the Taff Trail to Cardiff, but even after two spins around the bus station and a lengthy haul up some of the side-streets, nothing but a sign to NCN 47 was to be seen – and that pointed in the wrong direction for me.

Well, 'Pooh to Sustrans!' I thought. First you send me over the steepest roads in South Wales and now that there's a gentle off-road route to be had, you won't even tell me where it is! In something of a bad temper, I followed the ordinary road signs to Cardiff and suddenly found myself once again doing battle with the HGV brigade along the hard shoulder of the A470 dual carriageway, the trans-Wales road that I'd last seen in far-away Dinas Mawddwy. Even though the sign on the slip-road had definitely banned only horse-drawn vehicles and pedestrians, a number of motorists still hooted at me as I pedalled frantically – but steadily – in search of the nearest exit. It was about three miles away and I have since erased the memory of those three miles from my grey cells.

Eventually, I did manage to prise the Taff Trail from Sustrans's hidden vault, at Nantgarw, where a little wooden sign told me that Cardiff was only ten miles away – and then, after about 500 metres, only seven miles – a miracle! After two of those, it was declared as being still seven miles away and from this point I ignored the signs and simply enjoyed the ride. Very enjoyable it was too: a steady downhill gradient with ever-changing scenery, now a high old railway embankment, now a leafy riverbank, and now a paved path through an urban park. The Taff Trail is a fifty-five-mile route all the way from Brecon and mostly traffic-free, as on this stretch. For once, the marketing hype was actually true, for it claims that the trail's 'green fingers' bring the countryside into town and, even though I knew I must be approaching the city of Cardiff, I was surrounded for the most part by trees, hedges and views over green fields.

What distinguished this southern end of NCN 8 from the Lôn Las Cymru that I'd picked up by the Menai Straits and left in Machynlleth, was its traffic. With it being going-home time on the edge of a city of 300,000 people, it was the M1 of cycle routes. All sorts of cyclists passed by in the opposite direction: slick-clad athletes on drop-handlebar racers, smartly-dressed office types on shiny mountain bikes; slow, middle-aged women on creaky three-gear jobs, fast young women on sit-upright hybrids; uniformed children, hooded youths, helmeted fathers and families of three little helmets in a row. I take it all back, Sustrans: thank you for keeping these people off the roads and thank you for letting me watch them all shoot by.

After about an hour, the Taff Trail, which had been hugging the left bank of the river, finally cut across a pedestrian bridge to the right bank – and here I left it, at least until tomorrow, as I diverted across a small park and out onto Cardiff's Cathedral Road, where the many guest houses included the one Julie and I had booked. It was extremely elegant and its landlord was indeed just as Julie had described him over the phone: 'as camp as a field of tents'. He'd told her that our room was called, unofficially, 'The Bishop's Room', as it was here that a certain bishop always stayed on his frequent trips to Cardiff (Llandaff Cathedral being just up the street) and indeed its plush red furnishings did have a certain ecclesiastical flavour – even the tasteful nudes on the wall.

Although the bright lights of the city lay just a few streets to the south, it was late, we were both whacked and both had our tales to tell, and so we soon decamped just up the road to the excellent Beverley Hotel, whose food and drink were very acceptable and whose prices were literally about half what we expected. With a cheap bottle of Rioja to hand, our various tales were soon spilling out quite easily.

'We saw the storms in Wales on the news,' said Julie. 'My mother was worried about you being out on your bike, but I said you'd be sheltering.'

'Oh.'

'You did shelter, didn't you?'

'It wasn't as simple as that.'

'How simple is it to lock your bike up and walk into a pub?'

'Well…'

'Or even a bus shelter?'

Sensing imminent defeat, I changed the subject.

'And anyway, I nearly starved.'

'In Britain, during shop opening hours?'

I realised I was on a sticky wicket.

'Good wine this, isn't it? Cheers.'

'Cheers.'

In fact, subsequent reports revealed that in the worst-affected locations two inches (five centimetres) of rain had fallen in just three days. The most I was subsequently able to glean about Swansea Bay itself was that, during the twenty-four hours that included the storm, the average – average! – wind speed had been 45 mph.

The good news was that my back-up clothing had now arrived. The bad news was that, judging from the forecast for my final day, I was going to need it.

Day 20

The End of It: Cardiff to South Point

Having admired the breakfast room's cherubs (which I felt sure the bishop must appreciate too), I was on my way while the rain held off. No weather, however, would dampen my keenness to reach yet another extremity, albeit the last one, bringing my tour to an end. Final destination: Rhoose Point, just twelve miles away. First stop: Cardiff Bay.

Cardiff comes from Caerdyf ('fort on the Taff'), even though the modern Welsh is Caerdydd. I was surprised to learn that it's been the official Welsh capital only since 1955, although it was probably the largest town in Wales as long ago as 1300. However, its progress has been far from steady, having been devastated by both the Black Death and Owain Glyndŵr (who set the town on fire) and in the eighteenth century being only a fifth of the size of Swansea and smaller even than Neath.

Its hinterland turned the tide. First iron then coal trundled down the Valleys to Cardiff by road, canal and then rail. By 1871 it was once again the largest town in Wales, by 1888 the price of world coal was determined in the town's Coal Exchange and by the 1890s the port of Cardiff (including Barry) was, incredibly, the world's largest – by tonnage handled.

The waterfront has changed a little since then and I was keen to see it. My route took me once again along the Taff Trail, which I picked up on the opposite bank of the river to the Millennium Stadium. Now here's an odd thing. The stadium, constructed around four giant, ninety-metre masts, was the largest in the UK when it opened in 1999 and dominates both this stretch of the river and this part of town... and yet it appears in, of all things, a guide book called *The Hidden Places of Wales* (see Bibliography). Hidden from whom? By the way, one of the Millennium Stadium's lesser-known features is a machine in each of its bars that can pull twenty pints of beer in less than twenty seconds. It's known around here as a 'joy machine'.

Cardiff Bay is the new name for the old docks area since the tide has been kept out by a barrage, also built in 1999, which has created, according to its own marketing, 'Europe's most exciting waterfront'. Well, I guess it depends what turns you on. The place it most reminded me of was

– once again – Barcelona, with its new port area: bold new buildings joined to spruced-up old ones by expensive new paved areas. Just the weather reminded you this was Wales, as the bay itself reflected the grey-black sky and, by the time I'd cycled around the waterfront (that morning, possibly Europe's most deserted), its reflections were broken by raindrops.

The Taff Trail, and therefore the very last few metres of NCN 8 on its journey right across Wales, had deposited me near the mouth of the Taff as it emptied into the bay, and another Sustrans sign directed me over the Taff Bridge towards Llandough, before abandoning me like an out-of-favour rag doll on the other side. Left to my own devices, I quickly got lost in an apartment complex before taking what was almost certainly an illegal little path across the Ely Bridge. Did the Sustrans sign-placer go to lunch and never return?

Passing through the suburb of Llandough, I managed to catch a glimpse of the hospital, famous – according to the ever-resourceful *Encyclopaedia* – for having the longest corridor in Europe – and wondered how much of our taxes go towards funding the ECLMC (European Corridor Length Monitoring Committee)? By the time the main road delivered me into Barry, the rain had stopped.

Though the statistics that placed Cardiff as the world's number-one port included Barry, the two were for many years bitter rivals. By the 1880s, a number of coal-mining entrepreneurs were frustrated by the tidal restrictions in Cardiff Docks – and uneasy with the operational stranglehold of their owner, the Marquess of Bute – and so Barry Docks were born. Within twenty years, their coal exports actually exceeded Cardiff's and the man most responsible for their success is commemorated in a statue in front of the old Dock Office: David Davies. Sitting at his feet, I munched a couple of digestives from The Bishop's Room while surveying the scene.

The vast dock area which spread at my feet was mostly empty, but in the distance giant piles of pallets hinted at some continuing activity. Nearby, the requisite number of dockside apartments for 'dockside living', with their requisite number of yuccas, had been given their place in the sun, so to speak. Davies himself seemed to be comparing the scene with his original plans – and looked distinctly unimpressed.

For my part, I was quite impressed with Barry, actually. I passed through some posher suburbs with proud detached houses and dramatically luxuriant front gardens. They seemed to have been built on a small mountainside, whose gradient rose to a severe G5 to remind me that, although I was nearing its very edge, I was still in Wales.

I'd taken a gamble with my drive for the south point. The map suggested that a mile or two of main road could be avoided by cycling through Porthkerry Country Park – except that the short link between the park and the outskirts of Rhoose comprised an unsurfaced track not marked as a public right of way and a railway embankment that may or may not be breachable. The rain had resumed with a vengeance as I approached the railway, but even through the torrents I could see that getting to the other side would not be a problem, since, while I was on the ground, the railway was about thirty metres in the air, atop an impressive viaduct, across which a suburban service rattled as I squelched below. The track, though, was a different story.

In this weather, 'unsurfaced' meant quagmire and, as an extra hazard, the untended trees of the surrounding woods had closed off the space above the track to within a metre or so of the ground. Well, I wasn't going back now... and it was about time I used this hard hat for some purpose. So, head down and chin on handlebar, it was another case of 'Chaaaarge!'.

Squelch, bang, thwack, splash, thwack, squelch... plus a few more bangs, the odd bruised knuckle and a front wheel laced with twigs... and I was through. I found myself in front of a small country house, now a hotel, and one which I scurried past sharply, before the concierge called the cops. For a moment I thought he'd called the air force, as a deep roar passed through the low clouds just above my head, until I realised I'd emerged just beyond the end of Cardiff International Airport's runway.

After brushing myself down (a rather pointless exercise given the state of my clothes) and de-twigging Tetley, I pedalled calmly into a new housing estate, locked Tetley against a stile and set off on foot to Rhoose Point and my journey's end. The map shows quite clearly that, in the coast's long swoop around the Vale of Glamorgan, the southern tip is this rather blunt headland. What it doesn't show is that a thin strip of high, exposed land separates the cliffs from the village of Rhoose. Along this strip runs a footpath which, at this point, seemed as steep and challenging as anything the better-known Pembrokeshire equivalent might offer. Scrambling up a narrow, muddy flight of steps, I emerged on a wider section bounded by barbed wire on both sides and with the air of a concentration camp perimeter. Through the raindrops on my map case, I struggled to judge the actual location of my target by carefully comparing my position with the pools just inland – but I needn't have bothered. For just ahead was planted a simple metal sign, to be read while facing out to sea. It read:

> Vale of Glamorgan
> Borough Council
> RHOOSE POINT
> Most Southerly Point on
> Mainland of Wales

Well done, the Vale of Glamorgan Borough Council! What your colleagues in Monmouthshire, Anglesey and Pembrokeshire appeared to be ignorant of, had not escaped your own attention. Like any country, Wales has its extremities and this was the last of them for me.

> Extremities: 4
> Days: 20
> Miles: 567
> Punctures: 0

Well done, Tetley! As I couldn't bring him to the actual end point, I'd plucked my water bottle from his frame and brought it up onto the cliffs instead, grabbing a celebratory gulp as I donned my spectacles to look around before they became too rain-spattered.

Not what you'd call a pretty sight.

Beyond the sign stood a tall, mesh fence topped with barbed wire. Beyond that, the mud and grass dropped sharply away at the ragged-edged clifftop. Beyond that lay what the *Encyclopaedia* insists is the Severn Sea, but what everyone I know calls the Bristol Channel. That day, though, it could just as well have been the Trent and Mersey Canal for all I could see of it: a canvas of variegated greys filled the field of vision to the south, waiting in vain for any features to be filled in. Turning inland, I took in a view that was no more inspiring. A lower barbed-wire fence stopped walkers plummeting into a series of man-made pools, beyond which were piled mounds of builders' rubble and finally two rows of modern houses struggling to make the best of being built in such a bleak location.

Never mind. Success is success. This southernmost extremity may have been the dullest of the four (at least on that misty, damp day), but it was the most significant. A series of twenty short bike rides, each with its own highlights, had been merged into a long and spectacular one: a 567-mile route around Wales which, so far as I knew, no one else had done.

By this time my glasses had transformed into two small, wet kaleidoscopes and so, pushing them back into my pocket, itself wet inside and out, I took just a few haphazard photographs before squelching off again to recover Tetley before a local cycle-liberator took pity on him.

In France you can always arrange to meet a friend in any unknown town at the *Café de la Gare*, as there always is one. In agreeing to meet at Rhoose railway station, Julie and I had been slightly optimistic, as it was one of the modern, facility-free variety. She had, however, managed to park the Golden Toyota next to a bus shelter and there, after heaving Tetley into the car, I was able to peel off at least some of my soggy clothes, leaving the rest to drip from my body onto the bath towel that my ever-efficient, one-woman support team had carefully placed on the passenger seat as she drove us to the nearest pub. This turned out to be about three miles west, a splendidly quirky thirteenth-century inn called the Blue Anchor and it was here, after I'd done a delicate striptease in the gents and re-emerged in deliciously dry clothes, and during the demolition of two monster ploughman's, that we addressed the question I'd asked myself three cycling weeks before: is Wales really such a strange land?

The main point we conceded of course is that, by the very nature of being just tourists, we'd merely skimmed over the surface of Welsh society, touching it almost exclusively only where the tourist industry reaches out to do business with the visitor: hotels and guest houses, pubs, museums and shops. The few exceptions – Davies Sanitary, Glyn and Alwena, the odd talkative smallholder or enthusiastic passer-by – may or may not be typical of their fellows.

'Still,' said Julie, 'a few oddities do stand out.'

'For instance?'

'Well, there are still a lot of independent shops – I wish there were as many in England. And hotels. Everywhere we've stayed has been privately owned, hasn't it? And virtually everywhere we've eaten too.'

'What about the National Milk Bars?'

'Hardly a global brand. No, I think that's a big difference.'

'Yes,' I agreed. 'You can tell Welsh high streets are still packed with traditional independent shops from their names: Jones the butcher, Morgan the bookseller, Greasy Annie the chipmaker. I wonder what her real name is?'

'I think you've made her up.' She winked at me, and after a short pause said, 'What else makes this place strange, then?'

'Well, for one thing, most of the accommodation seems to be in foreign hands – English hands, usually. But maybe this is only recent. Nearly everywhere we've stayed seems to have changed hands in the previous two seasons.'

'Well they're doing a great job,' added Julie. 'Everywhere we've stayed has been so lovely.'

'Except…'

'Yes, except the one disaster. I wonder if the Welsh have given up on the hotel trade, and why?'

'No idea,' I admitted. 'Oh, one thing they haven't given up on – and which is a definite one-up on England…'

'What's that?'

'Their singing, of course'

'Singing? What singing?'

'You wouldn't have heard it in your comfy little Yaris but significant numbers of the locals still burst into song without even thinking about it. Not just the Monmouth barmaid I told you about, and the Dinas trolley girl, but pedestrians, gardeners, shopkeepers… after a long, lonesome spell…'

'Oh, here we go.'

'... after a lonely ride in the hills, I'd often descend to the background noise of not just birdsong but personsong as well.'

'You sure it wasn't you inflicting a Beatles medley on the locals?'

'I'll happily admit I often sing to myself on the bike, but my point is that here in Wales I felt unusually at home doing it.'

'OK. What else?'

'Well,' I continued, lowering my voice, 'When I turn up somewhere, like here for example, looking like... like the only beaver to survive a shark attack...'

Julie choked on her beer.

'Where would you find beavers and sharks together?'

'You know what I mean. Even when I'm in a right state, nobody in Wales seems to pay a blind bit of notice.'

'What do you want? Applause?'

'No! In England people at a bar would want to know how I'd got in such a state.'

'Maybe they're just more polite in Wales,' we both pondered this for a moment. 'Anyway,' she continued, 'we've definitely seen some pretty strange things here.'

For a while, we concentrated in silence on memorable examples (and our pickled onions) while listening to the two men at the bar debating the reliability of Ford Mondeos. Finally, I waved my fork in the air.

'There was something distinctly odd about those sudden plastic palm trees in Pant-y-dwr. And as for the minibus full of cow-girls in the middle of Cross Hands...'

'You did say you were looking for something exotic…'

'It's not the sort of exotic I was expecting.'

'But that's the point, isn't it?' pointed out my perceptive partner. 'Wales brings you the unexpected. Don't they do bog-snorkelling somewhere?'

'Llanwrtyd Wells. They have an annual race between horses and humans there too. Come to think of it, up in Caernarfon I found out they race against trains as well.'

'There you are then. It's the Land of the Unexpected.'

'Except the rain. I suppose I expected that.'

'You say you're a geographer – you certainly should have done.'

On reflection, even though I moaned about the wet and windy conditions when I was in the middle of them, I did just battle on through – whether it was a particularly bright thing to do or not. And that, I suspect, is a trait the English, Welsh and Britons in general share: we're a bit of an obstinate lot.

Wet or not, strange or not, Wales had provided me with an unforgettable and frankly invigorating cycle tour. Next time, though, I'll spend more on waterproofing.

Now, where does the rain fall in Spain?

Statto Corner

My route distance, calculated from maps and signposts rather than an odometer, was 567 miles (913 kilometres). The breakdown is as follows.

Day	From	To	Miles	Km	Comment
1	East Point	Monmouth	4	6	Excludes getting to the East Point.
2	Monmouth	Hay-on-Wye	34	55	
3	Hay-on-Wye	Llandrindod Wells	27	43	
4	Llandrindod Wells	Llanidloes	25	40	
5	Llanidloes	Bwlch y Groes	36	58	
6					Day off
7	Bwlch y Groes	Betws-y-Coed	34	55	

Day	From	To	Miles	Km	Comment
8	Betws-y-Coed	Menai Bridge	24	39	
9	Menai Bridge	Menai Bridge	46	74	Via North Point. Includes 2 miles on foot.
10	Menai Bridge	Porthmadog	29	47	
11	Menai Bridge	Aberdovey	45	72	Includes 4-mile diversion to Shell Island causeway.
12	Aberdovey	Aberystwyth	27	43	
13	Aberystwyth	New Quay	23	37	Includes 2-mile diversion to Llansantffraed beach.
14	New Quay	Eglwyswrw	25	40	
15	Eglwyswrw	St David's	27	43	
16	St David's	Narberth	33	53	Via West Point. Includes 1 mile on foot.
17	Narberth	Tumble	44	71	
18	Tumble	Briton Ferry	32	52	
19	Briton Ferry	Cardiff	40	65	
20	Cardiff	Rhoose Point (South Point)	12	20	
		Total	567	913	

Average distance per day: 28 miles (46 km)

Average cakes per day: 2.5

Cakes per day justified by 28 miles' cycling: 12

Marmalade sandwiches surreptitiously removed from guest-house breakfast rooms: 7

Flasks of coffee made from complimentary coffee trays: 2

Flasks of coffee made from complimentary coffee trays ending up in the ditch: 2

Rainy days: 10

Windy days: 10 (not exactly the same 10 as the rainy days)

Best day's cycling: Day 12 – Aberdovey to Aberystwyth

Worst day's cycling: Day 18 – Tumble to Briton Ferry

Best stretch: Tumble to Llanelli (part of NCN 47/Celtic Trail)

Worst stretch: A470 south of Pontypridd

Bike (Tetley): Triban Trail 7 from Decathlon

Brake blocks used: 4

Electronic navigational aids used: 0

Books carried for en-route reference: 3

Books actually referred to en route: 0

Punctures: 0

Highest point on route: Bwlch y Groes, Gwynedd (545 m)

Best accommodation (author's vote): Buckley Pines Hotel, Dinas Mawddwy

Best accommodation (support team's vote): Craig-Y-Wig Guest House, New Quay

Worst accommodation (joint vote): Narberth Disaster Inn (not its real name)

Best cake: Bara brith, Postgwyn Guest House, Eglwyswrw

The Ten Laws of Cycle Touring

1: What goes up must come down.
2: If it might rain, it will.
3: Know your kit.
4: Wind and gradient are effectively the same thing.
5: When you hit the lily pond, you're at the top.
6: Your map is your second-best friend (after your bicycle).
7: A padded groin is a happy groin.
8: Be diverted.
9: When you hit the dog-walkers, you're about to hit town.
10: The rain will eventually stop.

More 'Meanings of Liff'
from Wales

beguildy (Powys) (adjective) – beguiling on first appearances, but revealing a doubtful character soon afterwards.

burlingjobb (Powys) (noun) – a person who takes the credit for work done by someone else.

bont (Monmouthshire) (noun) – an unsuitable hat, e.g. a baseball cap worn by a man over forty.

chirk (Wrexham) (verb) – to slip off an object immediately after putting one's weight on it, e.g. a kerb or the arm of a chair.

domgay (Powys) (noun) – a game between two consenting adults, where one (the magor) must be at least two feet taller than the other (the kilgetty). Illegal in all parts of Wales except Merionethshire.

freystrop (Pembrokeshire) (noun) – used only in the phrase 'in a freystrop': temporarily unable to act, having been asked to do more than one thing at a time. Common in males.

kilgetty (Pembrokeshire) (noun) – see domgay.

knucklas (Powys) (noun) – a person who is so wide that the only way their arms can hang by their sides is with the knuckles facing forward.

llong (Flintshire) (noun) – a thong larger than size 18.

magor (Monmouthshire) (noun) – see domgay.

murch (Cardiff) (noun) – the gloopy liquid that develops at the bottom of a vinegar bottle if left untouched in the cupboard for two years.

narth (Monmouthshire) (noun) – the person who never leaves the kitchen at a party.

sketty (Swansea) (adjective) – irrationally mobile, especially the behaviour of insects when revealed under a stone: they go all sketty.

scurlage (Gower) (noun) – the detritus that gathers in a shower tray's plughole if not cleaned out for a week.

skenfrith (Monmouthshire) (noun) – a particularly bad case of 'sleep' in the eyes on waking, where the crunchy material spreads along the eyelashes.

solva (Pembrokeshire) (noun) – the soft, downy hair found on babies' heads.

splott (Cardiff) (noun) – a sound shorter than a splat, as of a fly swatted against a wall but too small to form a stain.

All these meanings are the inventions of the author and support team.

Select Bibliography

Books

Atkinson, David and Wilson, Neal *Wales (Lonely Planet Country Guide)* (2007, Lonely Planet Publications)
Adams, Douglas and Lloyd, John *The Meaning of Liff* (1983, Pan Books). All meanings offered here are not Adams and Lloyd's but the author's or Julie's.
Barnes, David *The Companion Guide to Wales* (2005, Companion Guides, Boydell & Brewer)
Borrow, George *Wild Wales* (1862, Collins)
Davies, John (and others, editors) *The Welsh Academy Encyclopaedia of Wales* (2008, University of Wales Press)
Gerrard, David *The Hidden Places of Wales* (2006, Travel Publishing)

SELECT BIBLIOGRAPHY

Websites

www.castlewales.com
Exhaustively detailed 'Castles of Wales's website

www.metoffice.gov.uk
Excellent website of the Meteorological Office

www.mtb-marathon.co.uk
Mountain-biking

www.ordnancesurvey.co.uk
Not just for maps but for the origins of Welsh place names

www.shellislandcampers.co.uk
Unofficial website for Shell Island, Llanbedr, Gwynedd

www.stayinwales.co.uk
Accommodation in Wales

www.sustrans.org.uk
National Cycle Network

www.theresposh.com
Unofficial website for National Milk Bars

www.visitwales.co.uk
Official Welsh tourist website

FROM THE MULL
TO THE CAPE

A GENTLE BIKE RIDE ON THE EDGE
OF WILDERNESS

RICHARD GUISE

FROM THE MULL TO THE CAPE

A Gentle Bike Ride on the Edge of Wilderness

Richard Guise

ISBN: 978 1 84024 674 2   Paperback   £7.99

Richard Guise yearned to take on a physical challenge before he reached the age where walking across the kitchen would fall into that category. And so he donned a cagoule, packed his saddlebags and set off for an adventure on a bike named Tetley. This is the tale of his 586-mile, 16-day ride through the Highlands of Scotland, along the dramatically beautiful west coast from the Mull of Kintyre in the south to Cape Wrath in the north.

Freewheeling along isolated roads where traffic problems consist of the occasional retreating sheep and stopping for lunch on deserted beaches, he has time to ponder the Laws of Cycle Touring and take in spectacular sights, from craggy, cloud-shrouded mountain ranges to lochside forests.

'... *the perfect companion for the traveller to the west coast of Scotland*'

FLIGHT magazine

'... *just might make you stir your stumps and get on your own bike*'

UNITE magazine

two feet, four paws

walking the coastline of britain

spud talbot-ponsonby

TWO FEET, FOUR PAWS

Walking the Coastline of Britain

Spud Talbot-Ponsonby

ISBN: 978 1 84024 738 1   Paperback   £7.99

Tackling treacherous paths and the unpredictable British elements, one headstrong dog and a feisty young woman set off to cover a distance equivalent to London to Kathmandu to raise money for charity. Walking the entire coastline of Britain, Tess the dog flirts outrageously with good-looking farmers and charms unsuspecting toddlers into parting with their ice creams. From sleepy fishing villages to unrelenting urban streets, meeting avocets and flamingos, Spud slows life down for a year and sets off to find herself along the way.

A fascinating read for anyone interested in walking and the British coast – the heart-warming tale of one dog and her owner, who face the daily challenges with a boundless sense of humour and determination.

'This book might just make you think twice about fleeing abroad'

Ffyona Campbell

THE
BIG WALKS
OF GREAT BRITAIN

including South Downs Way, Offa's Dyke Path, The Thames Path,
The Peddars Way and Norfolk Coast Path,
The Wolds Way, The Pembrokeshire Coast Path,
The West Highland Way, The Pennine Way

DAVID BATHURST

THE BIG WALKS OF GREAT BRITAIN

David Bathurst

ISBN: 978 1 84024 566 0   Paperback   £9.99

From the South West Coast Path to the Great Glen Way, from the Cotswold Way to Hadrian's Wall, and from the Yorkshire Wolds to Glyndwr's Way, there are big walks here to keep you rambling all year round. And what better way to discover the landscapes of Great Britain, from green and gentle dales to majestic mountains and rugged cliffs?

An indefatigable walker, David Bathurst has unlaced his boots to produce this invaluable companion to the 19 best-loved long-distance footpaths. His appreciation of the beauty and history of the British countryside and his light-hearted style will appeal to experienced and novice walkers alike.

'Meaty, practical guide jam packed with walks that promise to keep you rambling all year round'
                                        THE SUNDAY EXPRESS

'Should appeal to experienced and novice walkers alike. There are detailed descriptions of the trails and a wealth of practical information, including amenities'
                                        BLACKPOOL GAZETTE

Have you enjoyed this book? If so, why not write a review on your favourite website?

Thanks very much for buying this Summersdale book.

www.summersdale.com